# Basic Upholstery
## REPAIR AND RESTORATION

# Basic Upholstery

## REPAIR AND RESTORATION

Robert J McDonald

B T BATSFORD LTD *LONDON*

ISBN 0 7134 1821 4

Filmset by Latimer Trend & Company Ltd, Plymouth
and printed in Great Britain by
The Anchor Press Ltd, Tiptree, Essex
for the publishers
B. T. Batsford Ltd
4 Fitzhardinge Street
London W1H 0AH

# Contents

# Introduction

After writing two previous books on the craft of upholstery – *Upholstery Repair and Restoration* and *Modern Upholstering Techniques* – both dealing with their differing methods of application in some depth, I came to the conclusion that the next logical step was to produce a further book dealing with *both* aspects of the craft in a more simplified and concise way.

My aim in writing this additional volume is to produce a rather more condensed, but nevertheless understandable, version of my earlier works, omitting the amount of technical detail necessarily included in those books which are intended for the student, apprentice upholsterer and professional journeyman upholsterer.

I have at the same time attempted to include a broader range of more simplified upholstery projects with easy-to-follow instructions, drawings and photographs. In appropriate cases I have explained certain short cuts which are, for economy reasons, commonly employed by the professional upholsterer.

Also in writing this volume I have tried to cater for those who have not had any previous experience of upholstery work and who may be desirous or perhaps undertaking the re-covering or restoration of a favourite piece of upholstery for the fun and excitement of so doing, with the additional benefit, of course, of saving the cost of having the work done professionally.

I have also tried to keep in mind the reader who has been attending a needlework or embroidery group and who may now wish to put his completed needleworked, embroidered or perhaps woven tapestry panel to good use on a piece of upholstery in some way.

This book could prove equally useful to the woodworker, enabling him or her successfully to upholster a seating unit which may have been constructed for an upholstered finish.

I have, over a long period, visited innumerable handicraft shows and exhibitions of work produced by enthusiastic amateurs and have unfortunately seen many efforts at home upholstery which would have been greatly enhanced by a little professional advice, enabling their treasured hand-craft piece to be shown to greater advantage. It was with these points in mind that I put pen to paper once again to try to encourage readers to attempt the mysterious craft of upholstery. By following the instructions and advice given in this book, the reader may achieve an acceptably professional standard of work of which to be proud.

The first, and probably most important, piece of advice to give to readers prepared to undertake upholstery work from this book, is to have a great deal of patience. This is fundamental throughout – don't give up at your first efforts in disgust if what you are attempting does not go right.

A beginner will no doubt at first find some difficulty in achieving a neat and tidy appearance in the work, due to the problems involved in handling the materials, i.e. keeping fabric square and the threads straight, removing fullness, etc.

The work of upholstery consists of manoeuvring and moulding various fillings, materials and fabrics, which are all pliable, into the desired thickness and shape. Unlike working with wood, which is a solid commodity relatively easy to work with mechanical aids, the upholsterer has to be something of a sculptor in a simplified form – most upholstery is overcome by the deftness of the hands and an eye for a straight line or a pleasing aesthetic shape or curve.

One of the problems in writing about upholstery is trying to relate working instructions or drawings to a piece of work which may be in your possession. Unfortunately, there is such a vast array of past and contemporary designs or styles of upholstered chairs, etc., that it would be impossible to provide instructions or give information relating to every conceivable piece of upholstered work you are likely to undertake. But, I hope you will find instances in this book where an illustration, instruction, or drawing is relevant enough to your particular project to enable you to adapt the information given to suit.

# Tools

Fortunately, very few specialist tools are needed for home upholstery. A number of tasks may be undertaken with tools intended for other work, some of which may be readily to hand in many households. Tool requirements for upholstery work will differ somewhat, depending upon whether traditional craft work is being undertaken – in which case some specialist tools may be essential – or whether straightforward foamed upholstery work is being undertaken in the modern manner, when special upholstery tools generally are not needed.

## Non-specialist tools

### Hammers

A lightweight cabinet maker's pin hammer or something similar could be used in place of the standard upholsterer's hammer which normally has a small face of approximately 1.5 cm ($\frac{5}{8}$ in.). It is very difficult to do upholstery work with a large-faced, heavy hammer.

### Tacks

If working in the traditional way using tacks and hammer, it is useful to have a selection of sizes of tacks to work with. These should be 1 cm ($\frac{3}{8}$ in.), 1.3 cm ($\frac{1}{2}$ in.), and 1.5 cm ($\frac{5}{8}$ in.). The best quality, with most usable tacks with sharp points, are 'blued' tacks. Two types of tack are generally available – they are 'fine' tacks and 'improved' tacks (*diagram 1*). The 'fine' type has a slenderer stem and smaller head than its 'improved' counterpart. Generally speaking, the 'improved' type is for use with heavier timber or the more loosely woven types of materials.

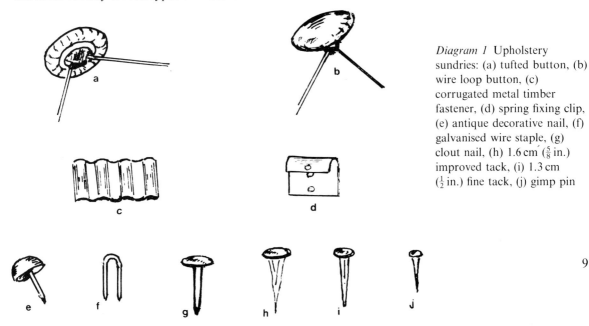

*Diagram 1* Upholstery sundries: (a) tufted button, (b) wire loop button, (c) corrugated metal timber fastener, (d) spring fixing clip, (e) antique decorative nail, (f) galvanised wire staple, (g) clout nail, (h) 1.6 cm ($\frac{5}{8}$ in.) improved tack, (i) 1.3 cm ($\frac{1}{2}$ in.) fine tack, (j) gimp pin

9

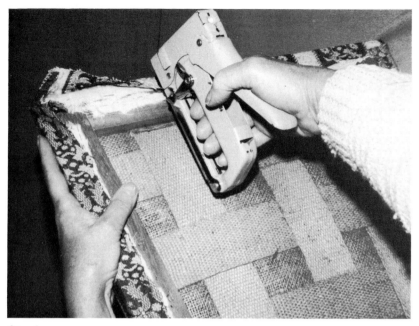

*Figure 1* Use of hand stapling gun for upholstery work

### Staples

As an alternative to the normal tacking of upholstery materials, a good staple-firing gun may be used to advantage – this will fire 1 cm ($\frac{3}{8}$ in.) or 6 mm ($\frac{1}{4}$ in.) wire staples into the timber. When purchasing a staple gun for upholstery work, ensure that it is sufficiently powerful to fire staples into hard timber, i.e. beech, and also that it is comfortable to work with (*figure 1*). Professional upholsterers mostly use compressed air-operated staple guns when working on modern production work, but as this is not practical for the home upholsterer a manual staple gun is the next best tool. Staples fired by the normal paper stapler will simply fold up and will not penetrate into the type of timber used in upholstery framework.

### Ripping chisel

When re-upholstery or re-covering is to be undertaken, the old covering should be removed completely. It is also frequently necessary to remove and replace the inner fillings, base canvas and webbing. This operation is normally carried out using an upholsterer's ripping chisel and mallet but, if these tools are not available, an old screwdriver and a cabinet-type hammer will do the work almost as well. It is not wise to use a new screwdriver as there is a possibility that the handle may be damaged by the continual knocking with the steel face of the hammer.

### Scissors

Cutting materials and trimming off surplus fabric used for upholstery require a fairly large sharp pair of scissors – the professional will use a pair with a size of 20 or 23 cm (8 or 9 in.). It is a great temptation to tuck surplus

10

material into the work but this practice often forms unsightly lumps and uneven lines in a finished job and it is much wiser to take the trouble to cut away *all* surplus materials right up to the tacking point.

*Needles*

If covered upholstery buttons are to be used in the upholstery, a fine buttoning needle 20 cm (8 in.) will be needed. A good quality flax or nylon twine should be used for this, threaded through the tuft or wire loop at the back of the button (*diagram 1a and b*) and through the base of the work (*diagram 2*).

*Diagram 2* Button tied down through base of upholstery with reinforcing 'butterfly'

## Tools for traditional style upholstery

Figure 2 and diagram 3 show tools required for traditional upholstery. Except for the stitching and buttoning needles, substitutes for other tools mentioned may be found:

**a** webbing stretcher
**b** upholsterer's hammer
**c** scissors
**d** spring needle
**e** fine buttoning needle
**f** upholsterer's regulator
**g** bayonet needle
**h** wood rasp
**i** leather knife
**j** hide or web pincers
**k** cabriole hammer

Two commodities also shown in the photograph in frequent use are:
**l** flax twine
**m** adhesive (Copydex)

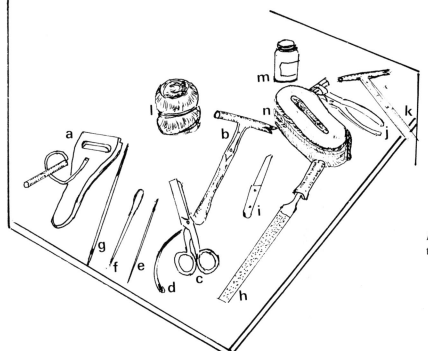

*Diagram 3* Tools required for traditional upholstery work

11

*Figure 2* Tools for traditional
upholstery work

**Webbing stretcher**

Figure 3 shows the method of threading webbing through the slot of the
normal 'bat'-type webbing stretcher. In figure 4 the webbing is being
tensioned by levering the narrow handle section down and holding it steady
approximately horizontal whilst tacking the webbing into position. Care
must be taken to ensure that the webbing is not over-tensioned as this could
damage the frame joints.

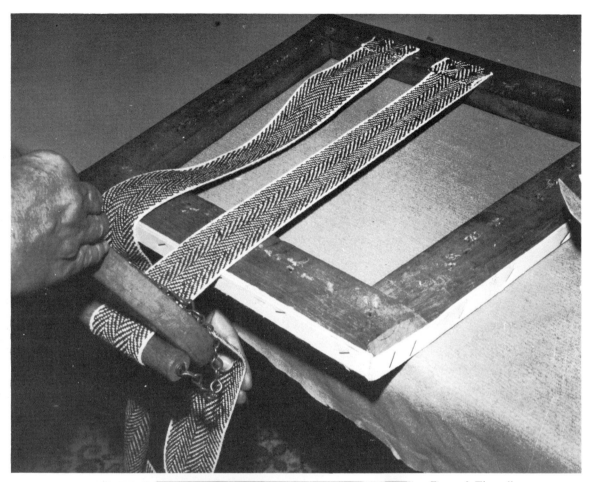

*Figure 3* Threading woven webbing on to the 'bat'-type webbing stretcher

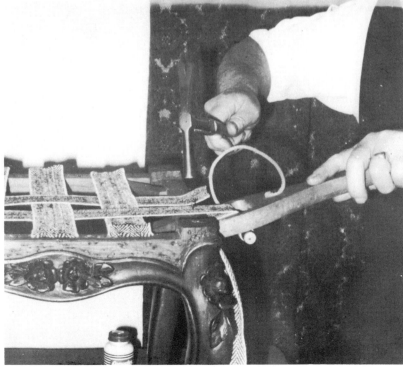

*Figure 4* Tensioning webbing using the 'bat'-type webbing stretcher

*Figure 5* Tensioning a strand of webbing over existing webbing using a piece of timber

Alternatively, if the 'bat'-type stretcher is not available diagrams 4a and b show a simple method of tensioning linen or jute webbing using a short piece of timber. The timber should be slightly wider than the webbing and approximately 14 cm (5½ in.) in length. By folding the webbing over the length of the piece of timber and tucking a fold into where the timber is bearing on to the frame, then gripping both firmly whilst levering downwards, you will achieve as good a tension to the webbing as with the normal tool. With a little practice, one can become quite adept at this operation (*figure 5*).

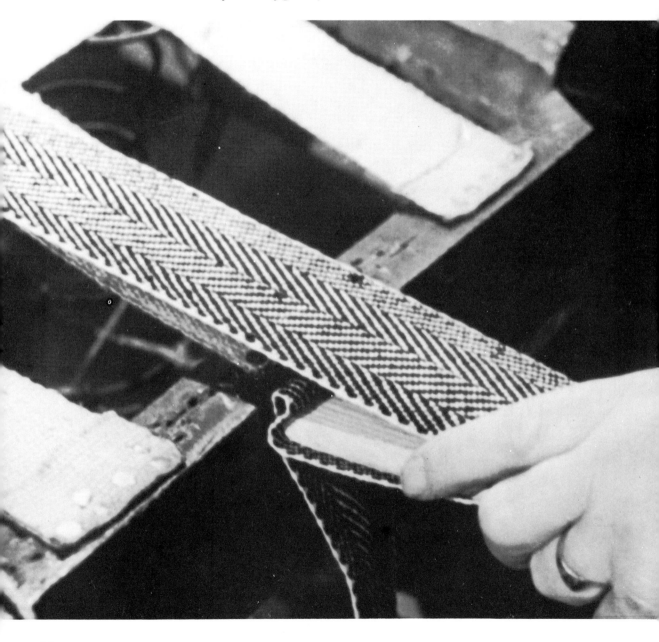

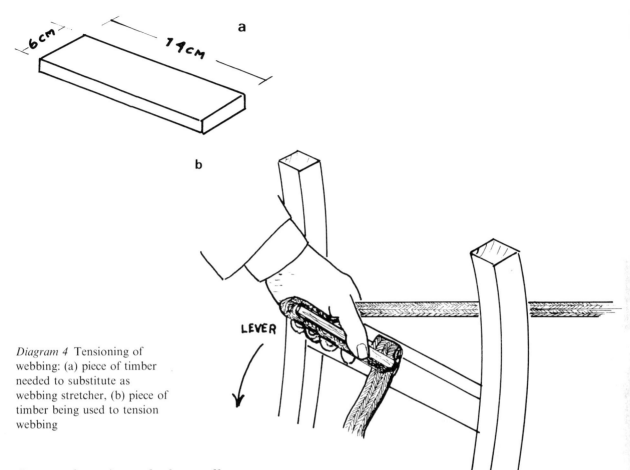

a

b

LEVER

*Diagram 4* Tensioning of
webbing: (a) piece of timber
needed to substitute as
webbing stretcher, (b) piece of
timber being used to tension
webbing

## Bayonet, buttoning and other needles

As mentioned a little earlier, unfortunately there are no practical
substitutes for the needles used by the upholsterer in the traditional
upholstery field. There are certain stages where these items are essential
(e.g. stitching of edge rolls on stuffed seats and backs, etc. is work for the
bayonet needle; stitching fine edges and deep buttoning is done with the fine
needle). These needles should be 20 to 25 cm (8 to 10 in.) in length for
normal stuffed work. The difference between the bayonet and the fine
buttoning needle is the triangular pointed end of the bayonet needle which
assists in opening filling, such as fibre, as it is being stitched. Also, being
stronger, it will withstand the considerable strain placed upon it whilst
stitching the rolls. A buttoning needle is a thinner gauge and is used to pass
through the tuft at the back of most covered upholstery buttons, although
some do have wire loops. A fine buttoning needle will also make a smaller
hole into leather or P.V.C. when pushed through with the twine to fix the
button in position.

A fairly stout curved spring needle has a variety of uses. In addition to
sewing coil springs on to linen or jute webbing, it is frequently used for
threading twine into the base canvas, an operation which is repeated many

15

*Diagram 5* 'Slip'-stitching of covering down side of chair back

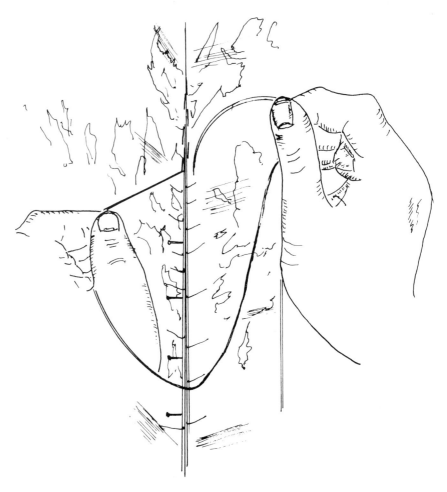

times. A further needle which will cope with a number of operations is a large semi-circular needle 15 cm (6 in.) in length; this can also take the place of the thicker spring needle and is easier to obtain. When purchasing the large semi-circular needle often a smaller one is attached to the card with it. A 7.5 cm (3 in.) semi-circular needle is necessary for 'slip-stitching' a covering (*diagram 5*).

### Hide pincers

Hide pincers or strainers are a help in the tensioning of hide or leather over the filling and assist in taking out the wrinkles caused by the contours of the filling and frame. A further use for this tool is the tensioning or taking out of the slackness from webbing which has been used for some considerable time and has bowed on the underside of the seat. By lifting the tacks at one end of the webbing, the wide jaws of the hide pincers will grip the width of the webbing and, by resting the flange of the underside of the tool against the frame and levering, a good tension can be obtained once again when the webbing is retacked, avoiding the original tack holes. Two sizes are available, the 5 cm (2 in.) width being more convenient and more useful for webbing than the 2.5 cm (1 in.) width.

## Wood rasp

A wood rasp, similar to a very coarse file, is very useful for reducing rough edges or protruding corners of framework which could cause damage to covering. This tool will quickly take timber edges down without recourse to a plane and it is particularly useful when a 'drop-in' loose seat is being recovered perhaps with a thicker fabric than the original covering (i.e. a piece of embroidered work or tapestry) which will cause the seat to be oversize.

Before applying the new covering the fit of the seat should be tested by slipping the new covering, or an off-cut, between the uncovered seat frame and the rebate into which the seat fits (*figure 6*).

It may be found that the seat frame will not enter the rebate. If this is the case, on no account force the seat into position as this action will most certainly damage the polished chair frame and force the joints open. The face edges of the loose seat are easily taken down the fraction needed with the use of a wood rasp.

Conversely, testing the loose seat may show that there will be a slight gap when the new covering is tested between the seat frame and the rebate – this would occur if the new covering is thinner than the original. In this

*Figure 6* Testing fit of seat using sample of new covering

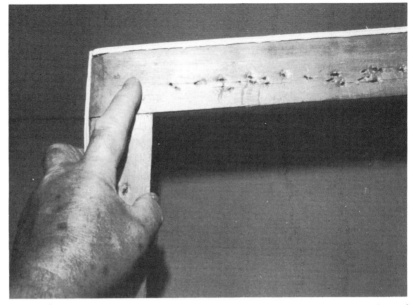

instance, a strip or two of card cut to the same width as the side member of the seat, then tacked into position on the edge, as shown in figure 7, using 1 cm ($\frac{3}{8}$in.) fine tacks is the answer.

### Knife

It is sometimes easier and more convenient to remove surplus fabric or leather covering with a knife than with a pair of scissors. A normal shoe repairer's leather knife is ideal for upholstery purposes, provided it is kept keen and sharp. The blade of a 'Stanley' knife tends to be too short and pointed for upholstery use.

# Materials

There is little difficulty in obtaining the materials required for contemporary style home upholstery. In the larger towns polyether foam (plastic foam), latex foam (foamed rubber), polyester fibre-fill (Dacron), resilient rubber webbing (Pirelli), and coverings of all types, including P.V.C. coverings, are all frequently on sale in specialist D.I.Y. stores and, indeed, in many shopping markets.

## Stuffing

Materials for the traditionally stuffed style of upholstery, i.e. jute and linen webbing, hessian (canvas), coil springs, twine, tacks, etc., are rather more difficult to obtain but are available in many areas in stores which are happy to supply commodities in small quantities suitable for the D.I.Y. home upholsterer. A number of such suppliers are listed towards the end of this volume. Further suppliers of upholstery materials are listed in the British Telecom's Yellow Pages.

It is feasible to re-use some of the traditional materials when refurbishing a piece of upholstery. In fact, in many cases some of the basic work may be left in place and only the surface layer may need disturbing. When deciding whether to leave in place or re-use webbing, hessian, etc., thoroughly examine its strength as the material may have deteriorated to such an extent that in a short while after re-use it may split away, and your hard work will have been in vain. Generally it makes good sense to replace if in doubt.

## Coverings

The purchase of covering materials needs some thought and fabric intended for curtaining seldom is suitable as upholstery covering. The fabric used on upholstered items is subject to considerable stress and friction due to the weight and movement of people sitting. A bad selection of covering material could prove costly and result in disappointment at a later date.

When purchasing fabric woven with a traditional motif, remember that the motif needs centring on the panel of upholstery it is placed upon. In most cases, to achieve this it will be necessary to use the half width of the fabric which normally will have a complete pattern (*diagram 6*) with a similar complete pattern across the other half width of the cloth.

Centring of patterns does frequently involve some wastage but is well worth the small extra outlay for the better appearance of the finished piece

*Diagram 6* Length of covering with 'repeat' of pattern showing two seats with identical motifs from width of fabric

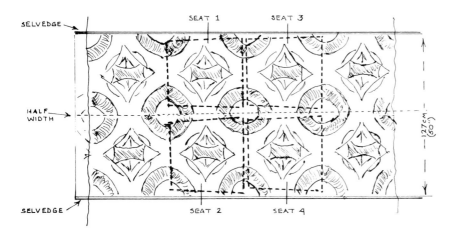

of upholstery. For the sake of economy and if the work being covered is small, it is an advantage to select fabric with a small repeating motif. A larger pattern will be partly shown only with possibly a good deal cut away to fit the upholstery.

Cloths which have been especially embroidered or woven are generally of a higher quality than normal production cloth so are suitable from the strength angle, but I have occasionally received a panel that was totally unsuitable from the point of view of shape and size for the upholstered piece it was intended to be used upon. So do bear in mind when first embarking on a panel of needlework what the end product is to be.

Woollen embroidered panels are frequently difficult to work as upholstery coverings because, although they are worked within a rigid rectangular or square frame, the work tends to go out of square when released from the frame. This is due to the tension of the stitches worked in certain directions. The panel will need to be straightened before it can be applied to a piece of upholstered work.

It is prudent to mark out and cut a paper or linen template or pattern of the exact size of the covering needed, to avoid under- or over-embroidering sides, front and back and, in particular, corners (which will generally need pleating) (*diagram 7*). Overlapping the thickness of woollen or other type of needlework would make the corners too bulky. Over-stitching sides, front or back could also prevent fitting of a seat snugly into the rebate of the base frame if it happened to be the 'drop-in' type of seat (*diagram 8*).

*Diagram 7* 'Drop-in' loose seat showing extent of embroidery necessary

*Diagram 8* Fitting of 'drop-in' loose seat

# Frames

Frames for upholstery work are normally made from the hardwood beech, the majority being constructed with dowelled joints (*diagram 9a*). Earlier period frames made use of the mortice and tenon joint (*diagram 9b*), these being hand constructed throughout, whereas present-day frames are mass-produced, cut and jointed mechanically.

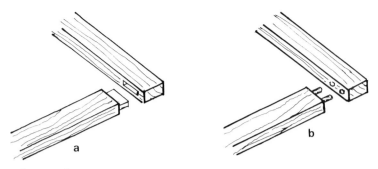

Diagram 9 (a) mortice and tenon joint, (b) dowelled joint

Timber frames for upholstery work are necessarily a fairly expensive item to purchase new, particularly for a 'one-off' job, due to the large amount of timber, shaping and labour involved. It is possible for the home craftsman to construct a fairly straight-membered chair frame as in diagrams 10 and 11 for example, but the more elaborate period style job is very difficult to prepare timber for and to cramp together without the appropriate cramps and jigs.

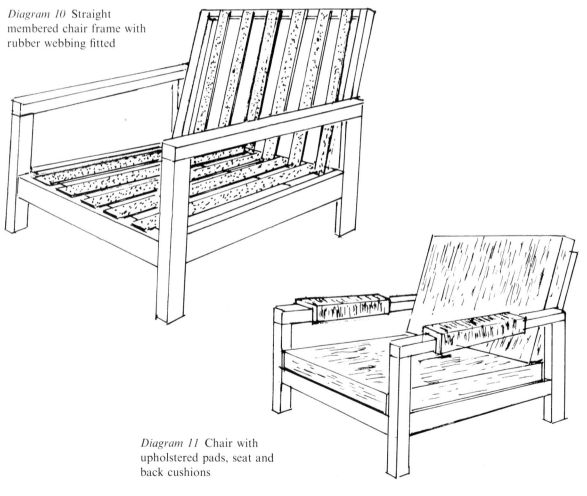

Diagram 10 Straight membered chair frame with rubber webbing fitted

Diagram 11 Chair with upholstered pads, seat and back cushions

## Repairs to frames

When the refurbishing of upholstered pieces is being undertaken, repairs to the timber frame often have to be coped with. In some instances joints will be found 'gaping' – this is when the glue has broken up and fallen away – or perhaps dowels may have broken. It may be necessary to knock both ends of a member apart to clean out the old glue and effect a repair. Joints which have been re-glued should be cramped using a suitable length sash cramp, or, if applicable, a 'gee' cramp. Figure 8 shows a recent innovation for the D.I.Y. repairer which involves plastic corner clamps, which are being held tight with a cord, pulling loose joints up tight. This gadget is readily available from D.I.Y. stores.

Figure 9 illustrates a very old-fashioned, but nevertheless successful, method of pulling together loose joints after they have been glued. Freshly glued joints should be left preferably 24 hours to allow the glue to cure completely. Animal glue used to be the only type used but there are currently a number of alternatives which are taking its place: P.V.A. is an easy adhesive to use and is one of the most popular.

*Figure 8* Use of 'Stanley' plastic frame cramps and cord to draw joints together

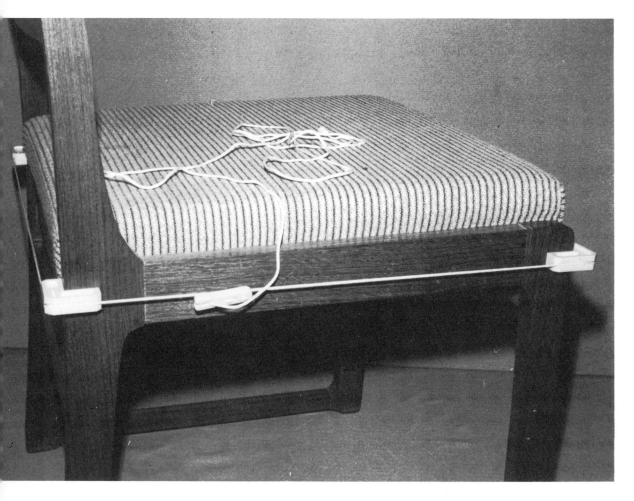

The use of flat metal jointing plates is to be recommended in a number of instances. These are ideal in situations as illustrated in diagrams 12 and 13. The advantage of using these plates is that they are quite flat when screwed into position and, if a layer of sheet wadding is laid over the plate and surrounding area, they are quite unobtrusive when the top covering is in position. These plates are generally available in most D.I.Y. stores. Diagram 14 shows a right-angled reinforcing piece of thin plywood cut to size and screwed over the slack joint of the frame; adhesive should be applied between the frame and strengthening piece using 1.3 cm ($\frac{1}{2}$ in.) screws to fix it into position.

*Figure 9* Tourniquet method of drawing joints together using cord and pieces of timber; polished finish at corners protected by card

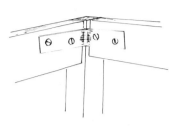

*Diagram 12* Internal, right-angled, steel reinforcing plate

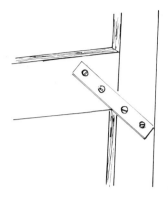

*Diagram 13* Straight, flat, steel reinforcing plate

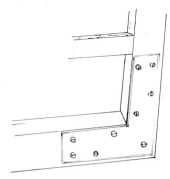

*Diagram 14* Plywood, right-angled reinforcing fillet

# Stripping upholstery

To avoid damage to the timber frame when stripping off old upholstery always rip the tacks out in the direction of the grain of the timber. Also, when nearing a corner of the frame, change the direction of working so that you work inwards from the corner towards the centre of the frame member. It is comparatively easy to split or chip a piece of timber away, particularly at corners, and any such damage to the frame will need to be made good. Care in stripping off materials pays dividends. Figures 10 and 11 show this operation in progress.

The original covering should not be left in place with the new covering tacked over it. Covering on most old pieces tends to be very dusty, grubby and often greasy, and any new covering applied over it will, within a short time, show signs of soiling on its surface.

As many of the original tacks as possible should be removed with the aid of the ripping chisel or old screwdriver. There may be a few obstinate tacks embedded deeper into the timber than the others. It is not vital that these be removed if they are too difficult, so do not risk damage to the frame, but hammer the offending tacks flat into the timber, after pulling or cutting the material away as close as possible so that it will not cause a proud spot under the new covering.

Holes which are left in the bare timber after removal of the tacks may look unsightly but do not worry about them. Clean away the short splinters which no doubt will be protruding, by using the wood rasp or a piece of coarse glass-paper. This will avoid the danger of splinters in the hands.

*Figures 10 and 11* **Ripping** tacks out along length of grain and away from corner using old screwdriver and mallet

When re-tacking the new materials it is easy to avoid the original tack holes – there is no need to fill them. For economy reasons it is tempting to try to re-use the old tacks which have been removed, but very rarely is it possibly to do this as most will be bent, damaged and rusty. It is best to discard them all and, from the outset, be prepared to proceed with a supply of new tacks of suitable sizes. Tacks required generally will be 1 cm ($\frac{3}{8}$ in.) fine tacks for top and under covering on the smaller items of upholstery with light timber members, 1.3 cm ($\frac{1}{2}$ in.) fine tacks for webbing and hessian, again on light types of upholstery framework, and 1.5 cm ($\frac{5}{8}$ in.) improved tacks for heavier items with thicker timber, e.g. for fixing webbing to the base of easy chairs, settees or couches, and spring hessian and coverings on to heavier members. It is impossible to describe the size of tack for each possible operation but the basic principle is to use the tack size which will not split the timber but is sufficiently large to hold the material being worked.

When working on smaller items it is convenient to work upon some form of table or bench, preferably not with a polished surface as, in addition to damaging the surface, the work will tend to slip around.

The operation of stripping using the ripping chisel and mallet or hammer of course requires two hands, so the item being worked upon needs to be held steady. In the absence of a further pair of hands, figure 12 shows a method of holding a seat steady.

*Figure 12* Loose seat held steady with pieces of webbing temporary tacked around frame

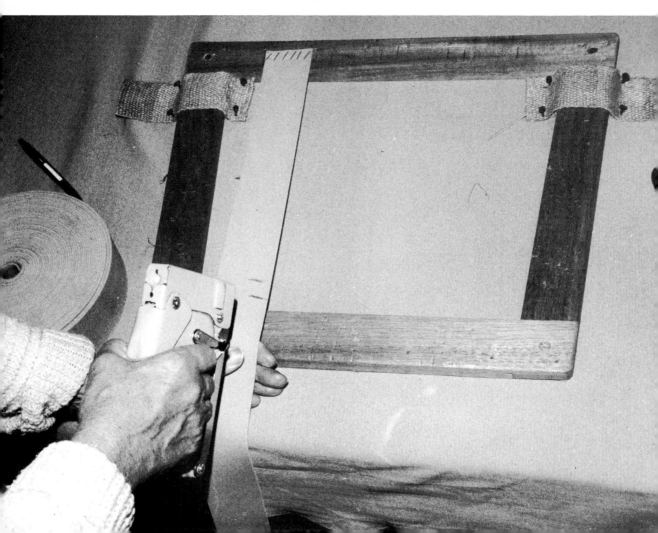

Staples, frequently used now for fixing coverings, etc. on modern upholstery, are notoriously difficult to remove if they have been inserted from a powerful compressed air stapling gun. Staples from such guns are often sunk well into the material and timber. Special staple-extracting tools are used by the professional upholsterer, but even with these tools there is often some difficulty in the removal of the staples. In most cases the materials being held by the staple can be prized away with the aid of a narrow-bladed, sharp screwdriver or, alternatively, a strong, pointed instrument – the upholsterer's regulator is a suitable tool which will do this job. As with tacks which are obstinate, if the staples are in too deeply to be removed, leave them in the timber after removing the material that was being held (*figure 13*).

Re-covering only an upholstered piece presents few problems. Once the original covering has been removed, this can be used as a template for cutting the new covering.

*Figure 13* Removal of staples using screwdriver with narrow sharp blade

Unfortunately, one cannot tell from outward appearances without a certain amount of experience what the condition of the interior will be like when the outer covering has been removed. It may transpire that you will need to do more than a re-cover job. Do not get carried away when stripping – some of the original basic upholstery may still be in good condition. It is often far better to leave the interior work undisturbed if possible, particularly if it is a rather ambitious project.

# Use of foam

Polyether foam and latex foam are a boon to the D.I.Y. home upholsterer. As pre-formed interior fillings, they obviate the need for loose fillings (such as horse hair and fibre, coil springs, etc.) as used in the traditional style of upholstery and most of which are somewhat difficult for the inexperienced upholsterer to control and use. Problems arise with loose fillings in attaining a suitable depth and density of the hair or fibre and with the shaping and stitching. The use of one of the foams overcomes these hurdles.

When working with foam great care must be taken in tailoring it, i.e. when cutting. Cuts should be smooth, upright and square. Jagged edges should be avoided as badly cut foam will invariably show in some way through the outer covering of the finished work.

## Cutting foam

Foam is easily cut with a broad-bladed, sharp knife, such as a bread knife or carving knife (*figure 14*). There is no reason why the D.I.Y. enthusiast cannot produce an acceptably professional appearance in the work he undertakes provided care is taken with the tailoring of the interior foam and the outer covering.

Foam cut for cushions should be cut slightly larger than the finished covering size. A normal seat or back cushion interior foam filling should be cut oversize by 6 mm ($\frac{1}{4}$ in.) on all four sides. The border width of the covering should be a little narrower after machining than the thickness of the foam interior, i.e. 6 mm ($\frac{1}{4}$ in.).

The oversize of the foam will ensure that the outer covering will retain a slight tension and avoid a wrinkled appearance. Care must be taken not to have the interior foam *too* large as this would cause bowing of the foam inside the outer covering.

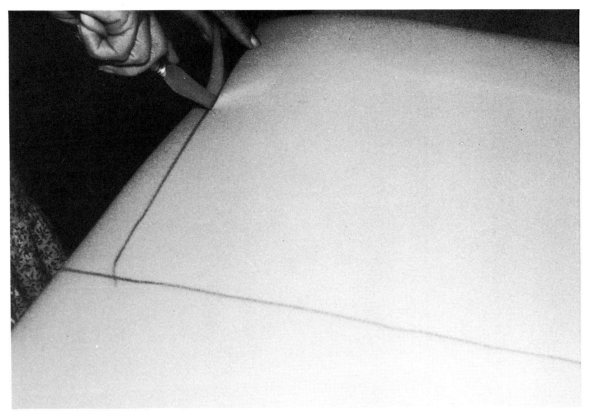

## Types of foam

A choice of types of foam, each having differing characteristics, is available for the interiors of such things as seat squabs, hassocks, seat and back cushions and normal upholstery use.

### *Latex foam*

Latex foam is made from natural rubber, foamed to give resilence and lightness. Latex rubber foam is available in a number of forms. Pincore latex (*diagram 15a*) probably now has the widest use in the latex field. Cut from a large block of foam, it can be supplied in stock thicknesses from 2.5 cm (1 in.) to 10 cm (4 in.). It can be easily cut by knife, due to its method of moulding with the small pencil-like cavities, and edges remain relatively smooth after cutting.

*Figure 14* Cutting sheet foam using long, sharp carving knife

*Diagram 15* (a) pincore latex foam, (b) cavity sheet latex foam, (c) moulded latex cushion

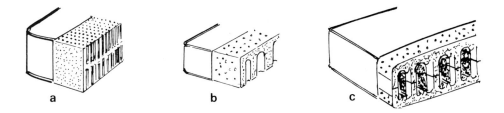

a            b            c

29

Latex foam is renowned for its resilence and recovery after compression, but tends to be the most expensive to purchase. Latex will cut more easily if the blade of the knife being used is moistened with water.

A further type of latex foam which has been rather ousted by the popularity of pincore is cavity sheet latex. This has a number of square or circular holes or cavities on the underside with a smooth top surface. This type of construction of the sheet foam makes it virtually one-sided if used as a single sheet (*diagram 15b*). Two sheets placed together with the cavities faced together will form a reversible cushion, but will need the addition of 'walling' made from slabstock latex. Slabstock rubber sheet is foamed rubber in thicknesses of 1.3 cm ($\frac{1}{2}$ in.) or 2.5 cm (1 in.). The 1.3 cm ($\frac{1}{2}$ in.) slabstock rubber would be cut in pieces to fit the sides of a cushion made from cavity foam where the cavities have given uneven and rough sides to the cut shapes. The 1.3 cm ($\frac{1}{2}$ in.) walling is then stuck around the sides giving a smooth finished face to a cushion. In production, latex cushions generally are moulded to size in two halves using the cavity principle, the two halves then being taped together around the face sides (*diagram 15c*).

Generally pincore latex foam is more convenient because of the smoothness of the cut edges which do not need walling after being cut.

### Polyether foam

Unlike latex foam which is a natural material from the rubber tree, polyether foam is produced by the mixture of chemicals causing 'gassing' which has a direct relationship with the hardness and density of the foam, this being dependent upon the formation of air cells within the foam.

It is *most* important to use a suitable density when working with polyether foam as there are a number of different grades of density and hardness. Foam used for seating purposes should be of a good firm density and of a seating quality, to avoid collapse or reduction in depth after a short period of use. Foam used for back cushions or back upholstery may be of a much lighter or softer grade as this takes very little strain or weight. Using a light density foam for a seating application will let the sitter down on to the front edge rail of the seat, making prolonged sitting very uncomfortable and causing 'pins and needles'.

### Reconstituted foam (chip foam)

An additional type of foam in the 'plastic' field is known technically as reconstituted foam. Produced under a number of trade names this foam is made from small granulated foam chips being mixed in with the normal foaming agent and moulded into sheet form. The resultant foam sheets can be worked as normal foam but this has a firmer and less resilient reaction. 'Chip' foam, as this type of foam is commonly called, is useful in various ways when a less yielding surface or edge is required (*diagram 16*). It is ideal for the interior padding of such items as chair squab cushions or kneeling hassocks, etc. (*diagrams 17 and 18*). This foam may also be sandwiched between layers of softer foam (*diagram 19*), or used with one softer surface layer to give an upper surface softness with a firmer base, perhaps for

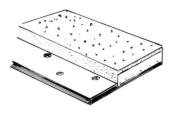

*Diagram 16* Reconstituted or 'chip' foam on plywood base

*Diagram 17* Chair seat squab with chip foam filling

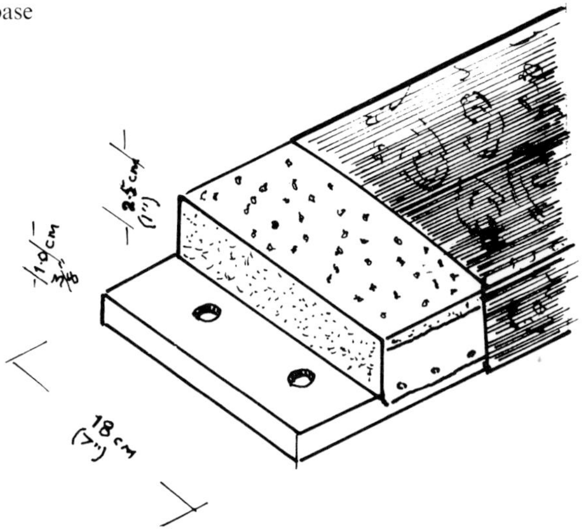

*Diagram 18* Kneeling hassock with chip foam filling on plywood base

*Diagram 19* Chip foam layer sandwiched between two layers of normal polyurethane foam

*Diagram 20* Seat base with double density foam layers

upholstery on a solid wood base (*diagram 20*). Figures 15 and 16 show examples of embroidered church kneeling hassocks.

A further use for 'chip' foam is the 'walling' of soft foam when leather or P.V.C. covering is to be used. This will give added resistance to the edges of the soft foam and prevent collapse with the tensioning of the leather or P.V.C. (These materials generally need more tension to prevent a wrinkled appearance.) (*Diagrams 21 and 22.*)

Figure 17 shows a circular seat squab with thin foam filling for a cane stool. To enable the circular shape to be maintained, plastic-coated curtain wire was used in the bias piping in place of the normal piping cord.

*Figures 15 and 16* Kneeling hassocks with embroidered motif coverings with filling of reconstituted foam

*Figure 17* Circular squab cushion for cane stool

*Diagram 21* Foam seat with firmer chip foam edging

*Diagram 22* Circular stool seat upholstered with foam, with reinforced chip foam edge

# Upholstered stools

The upholstery of a stool of some kind is a reasonably simple project to undertake for the uninitiated. The illustrations given here show a number of differing types of timber framed foot, kneeling and sitting stools of various sizes. The upholstery of a foot or kneeling stool should be firm with very little resilience. The work should be 'top stuffed', e.g. the filling should be applied to the upper/top surface of the frame.

*Figure 18* Foot stool frame for foam upholstery

## Simple stool upholstery *( figure 19 )*

Use black and white linen webbing or the cheaper brown jute webbing which should be tacked as shown in diagram 23, using 1.3 cm ($\frac{1}{2}$ in.) fine tacks with an overlay of hessian or canvas tacked singly and folded over after again using the same size tacks as for the webbing. The canvas will prevent the foam which we are to use in this project from being forced between the gaps in the strands of the webbing.

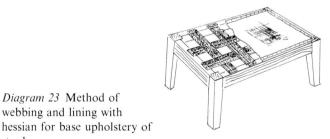

*Diagram 23* Method of webbing and lining with hessian for base upholstery of stool

*Figure 19* Foot stool with embroidered Florentine pattern

## Using foam

There are alternatives in proceeding with the remainder of the upholstery. A fairly firm density or even 'chip' foam may be used over the webbing and hessian, the foam cut slightly oversize of the width and length of the webbed and lined top. The covering can then be laid over and tensioned by tacking on the underside. The disadvantage of this method of upholstering is that when the covering has been given the correct tension across the surface and down the sides, the foam around the upper edges will have compressed almost down to the timber on the outer edge of the frame. This would give a very hard edge which would cause the covering to wear with abrasion and very soon to become threadbare.

*Figure 20* Altar kneeling stool with embroidered covering on upholstered loose seat

35

*Figure 21* Dressing stool upholstered with foam on plywood base

Diagrams 24 and 25 show methods of softening the edge: diagram 24 by tacking rubber draught excluder around the top edges, and diagram 25 by forming a tack-roll around the perimeter of the frame. The tack-roll may be filled with any form of loose upholstery filling, such as horse hair, fibre, shoddy or felt (*see figure 37 on page 53*). Strips of foam may also be used by rolling them firmly into the hessian, folding the hessian under and tacking the fold along the top edge about half way across the width of the rail. The tack-roll will provide a firmer edge than the surface foam will give and prevent the covering from wearing thin through abrasion on the harder edge (*see figures 38 and 39 on pages 54–5*). A suitable thickness piece of foam should be laid on the base hessian so that it fits inside the tack-roll; there will be no need for fixing – the tack-roll will contain it. A further piece of foam should then be cut so that it will fit over the upper surface and part way down the sides so that any unevenness along the length of the tack-roll will be smoothed out by the foam cover. The covering can now be laid over and tacked on the underside. Corners should be treated as in diagram 26a and b, pleated and slip-stitched (*see diagram 5 on page 16*).

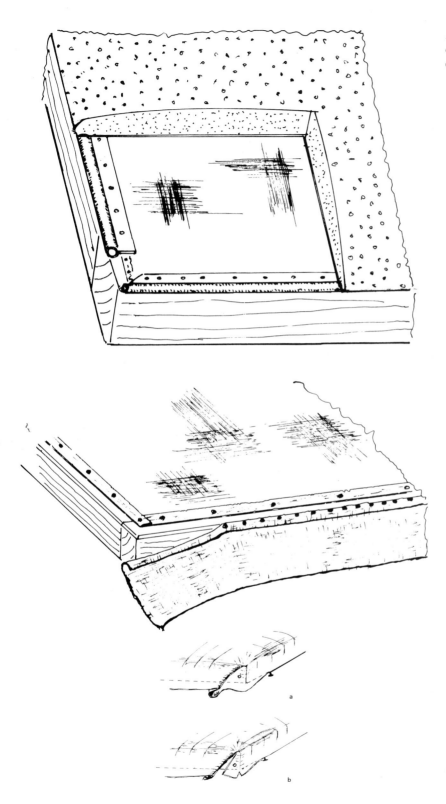

*Diagram 24* Use of rubber draught excluder to soften edge of timber

*Diagram 25* Tacking of hessian on edge of seat for tack-roll

*Diagram 26* Pleating covering at corner of 'drop-in' seat (a) stage 1, (b) stage 2, with covering finally tacked on underside of frame

*Diagram 27* Traditional upholstery of foot stool

*Figure 22* Dressing stool with deep buttoned seat, traditional upholstery

### Using loose fillings

An alternative method of upholstery for such a stool is stuffing with horse hair or fibre, and stitching (*diagram 27*). Again, this is worked upon the upper edge of the frame. The webbing and lining with hessian stage is as described on page 34 and the following sequences are as described for the upholstered seat in figure 19 and diagrams 34 and 35 (*see page 58*).

It will be noted that the covering material is tacked on the underside of the frame. There are two methods of doing this: (a) with the material folded under and tacked, which is a rather difficult operation, particularly with a thick covering such as wool embroidery or tapestry or similar material; or (b) tacked on the underside of the frame with a raw edge which is finally covered by tacking a piece of plain lining or some such material over the base with its edges folded under, using 1 cm ($\frac{3}{8}$ in.) tacks.

### Period foot stool with embroidered covering

Figures 23 to 26 show the simple construction and finished appearance of a period style cabriole-legged foot stool which has been trimmed with fringe.

Foam padding is used on chipboard with rubber draught excluder as edging as in diagram 24. Side members 5 cm (2 in.) wide are screwed to the underside of the chipboard, the cabriole legs are glued and screwed to the base of the side members, as in figure 25. Decorative moulding was used around the base of the side members in the example shown, but this can be omitted if desired.

*Figure 23* Embroidery being worked for period style foot stool

*Figure 24* Materials to construct period style foot stool

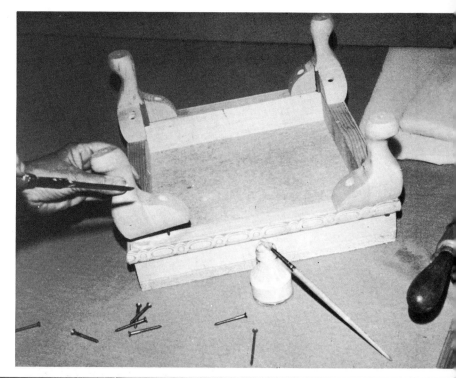

*Figure 25* Making up foot stool frame

*Figure 26* Completed foot stool with fringe trimming

# 'Drop-in' loose seats

An item of upholstery most frequently attempted by the novice must be the 'drop-in' seat, so called due to the method of construction where the chair seat is made as a separate unit to fit accurately into a rebate (recess) of a polished main frame (*figure 27*).

*Figure 27* 'Elbow' or 'carver' chair with drop-in loose seat

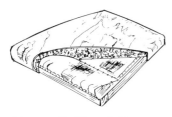

*Diagram 28* 'Drop-in' loose seat with padded roll along front edge

*Figure 28* Numbering on underside of loose seat

Early types of chair in this form were frequently stuffed with horse hair with the seats having a thick, bold front edge thinning down to the back edge of the seat as in diagram 28. These seats were generally retained in position by a dowel peg standing proud in the centre of the top edge of the front rail, with a hole to accept the peg in a corresponding position in the loose seat frame. As there was no rebate for the seat to be accommodated, the upstanding peg was necessary to hold the seat in position.

You may well have one or even a set of chairs with seats made in this form in your possession. In most cases where sets of chairs are still complete, each seat will carry a number on its underside to correspond with a similar number on the chair frame. This number enables the original fitting of the seats to be maintained throughout the life of the chairs. When refurbishing seats such as these, the numbers on the seats and chairs should be noted and indicated again on the underside of the seat on completion of the re-upholstery (*figure 28*).

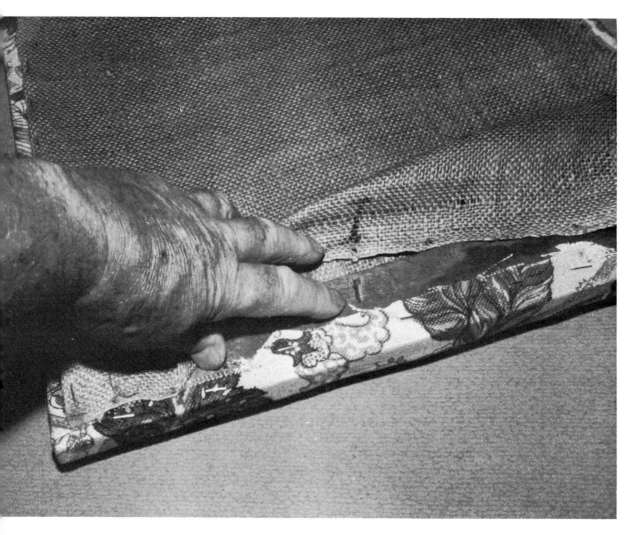

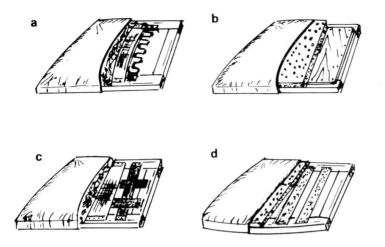

*Diagram 29* (a) seat with serpentine springing, (b) seat with plywood base and foam filling, (c) seat upholstered with woven webbing and horse hair, (d) shaped seat with rubber webbing and foam filling

## The modern method

The modern counterpart of the 'drop-in' loose seat is now manufactured in a variety of simplified ways for economic and mass-production reasons. The use of plywood, hardboard, rubber webbing, sinuous springing, foam, etc. has reduced the degree of highly skilled technical aspects of the work that were once needed to produce a high-class product. Diagrams 29a, b, c and d illustrate some methods of upholstery currently employed in producing the present-day dining chair seat.

You may recognize your own particular example of seat which you intend to re-cover or refurbish in one of these diagrams and, in some cases, one method can be changed for another, as illustrated.

### Plywood base

Drawing 'b' shows a seat frame with a plywood base nailed to the outer frame. Frequently this plywood becomes damaged, often by being stood or jumped upon which causes the plywood to split and makes the seat unserviceable. This damaged plywood is easily removed and replaced with a new piece cut to a similar size or, alternatively, it may be replaced with jute or linen webbing using $3 \times 2$ strands, or strands of resilient rubber webbing using the 3.6 cm ($1\frac{1}{2}$ in.) or 5 cm (2 in.) width. A base of webbing of either kind is preferable to a plywood base, proving to be more resilient and better for comfort (*figures 29 and 30*).

Foam used over a plywood base should be of firm density cut fractionally oversize. In all cases foam will tend to reduce slightly in size when being worked, so a wise precaution to avoid the outer edges of the timber being bare after covering is to overcut slightly.

*Figure 29* Linen webbing
tacked in position on loose
seat

*Figure 30* Resilient rubber
webbing tacked on loose seat

If the loose seat is of the completely flat type, an additional smaller piece of foam should be cut and placed centrally under the main piece as this will give a degree of doming and extra softness and depth to the upholstery (*figure 31*). Diagram 29d shows a concave-shaped seat frequently found, sometimes being concave in the front member only and sometimes with the shaping on both front and back members. In this instance care must be exercised to retain the shaping in the finished upholstery, particularly on

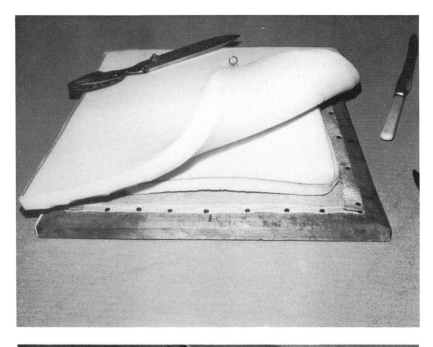

*Figure 31* Additional layer of foam in centre to give doming to surface of seat

*Figure 32* Trimming top edge of main foam to reduce thickness at sides

the front of the seat. Over-filling, or folding the foam under, will result in the concave shaping being spoilt and not matching the shaping of the polished base frame. Figure 32 shows the trimming of the top edge of the main foam to reduce thickness at the sides.

As mentioned in an earlier section (*figure 6*) check on the fit of the seat using the new covering before fixing the covering into position as adjustment may be necessary.

### Sinuous springing

A further method of loose seat upholstery is using a type of spring suspension, popular with chair manufacturers in recent years (*diagram 29a*), known as sinuous or snake springing. A small seat would generally have three strands of this type of springing consisting of black lacquered wire formed into a continuous series of 'U' bends. In the main, this springing is very reliable with little to go wrong with the strands other than the occasional faulty metal retaining clip which holds the end of the spring onto the frame. Occasionally one of these retaining clips may fracture, or perhaps the nail fixing the clip to the frame will work itself out of the timber. This fault will become apparent either by the uneven surface over the seat or when length of spring is seen curled down under the seat.

This fault may well occur in a larger piece of upholstery, perhaps an easy chair or settee seat, where one or more sinuous springs may become detached generally from the front rail fixing and be seen to be pushing out the bottom covering from its normal flat appearance (*figure 33*).

The remedy for a faulty or broken spring retaining clip, in the absence of a new clip (which you may often not be able to obtain), is to loop a piece of webbing around the last side of the end 'U' and tack the webbing where the clip was originally fixed, tacking with 1.3 cm ($\frac{1}{2}$ in.) tacks (*figure 34*).

There may be some difficulty in attempting to reposition these springs on the longer lengths, as used on easy chair or settee seats, due to the strength of the strand of spring, as it will curl naturally. This can be overcome by looping a length of cord or webbing around one of the sides of a 'U' section and straining the spring firmly towards the front fixing position until the spring is in position (*figure 35*). This operation may be difficult without help. Whilst tensioning the spring and holding the position the webbing needs to be tacked by an assistant.

*Figure 33* Detached end of spring protruding below seat

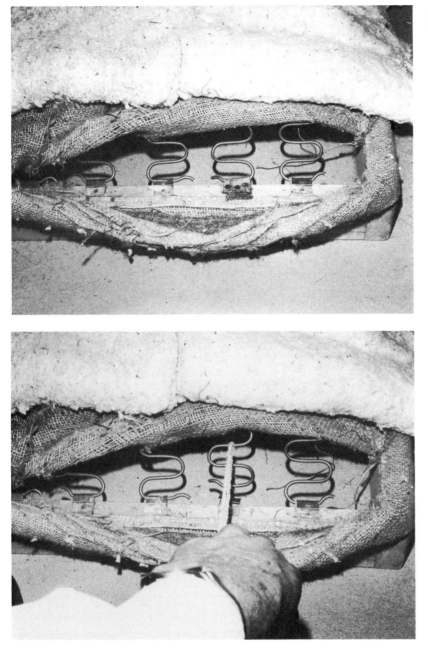

*Figure 34* Refixing loose
spring with webbing and tacks

*Figure 35* Method of straining
spring back into position

## Traditional method

A number of readers may find satisfaction in the re-upholstering of the 'drop-in' loose seat using traditional fillings and working in the traditional method, especially if the original seat or seats were upholstered in that way. Diagram 29c shows a cut-through section of a typical old-fashioned seat which, unlike its modern counterpart, has linen or jute webbing instead of plywood to support the filling.

### Webbing

The number of strands of webbing required on a seat depends upon the size of the seat frame, i.e. the area to be supported. Generally, the seats for 'carver' or 'elbow' chairs are larger than the normal 'small' chair, so, whilst $3 \times 2$ strands should suffice for the smaller seats, $3 \times 3$ strands should be applied to the carver seats. 1.3 cm ($\frac{1}{2}$ in.) fine tacks should be used for the fixing of the webbing.

Using the webbing strainer, or, alternatively, the piece of timber as shown in diagram 4a, care should be taken not to overstrain the webbing, as mentioned earlier. This is most important because, in addition to the risk of damaging the joints of the frame, the seat frame could develop a twist which will prevent it sitting flat and squarely into the base frame rebate.

### Hessian and filling

Over the webbing, hessian (canvas) should be tacked taut across with a fold *over* after being tacked singly using 1 cm ($\frac{3}{8}$ in.) improved tacks which are suitable for this stage. Do endeavour to keep the weave of the hessian in line with the front and back members – this should be easy if tacked first along the back member of the seat. Should the sides of the seat taper towards the rear, let the weave run off equally at each side. In all cases all woven materials will be easier to apply and manage if the weave is running parallel with the sides, back and front of the frame.

Any form of loose filling (such as horse hair, etc.) which is frequently found in the earlier upholstered loose seats will need twine ties to hold it in position whilst being worked. These ties, known as bridle or bridling ties, are inserted into the base hessian with a curved needle, such as a spring needle or large circular needle. To form the bridle ties, one end of the twine is knotted into the hessian first, approximately 7 to 8 cm ($2\frac{3}{4}$ to 3 in.) from a corner, then is run parallel to the frame side, forming loops by passing the twine through the hessian and out again so that the loops overlap each other by approximately 3 to 4 cm ($1\frac{1}{4}$ to $1\frac{1}{2}$ in.). The twine loops should run around each side at the same distance from the edges with two on each side and one down the centre in one direction only. The loops should be left a little slack – sufficient to slide in your hand to enable the filling to be tucked under and held in position (*figure 36*).

### Undercover

After the filling has been spread over the seat evenly with a slight doming in the centre, an undercover of cheap, unbleached calico or lining should be positioned over it. The undercover should first be temporary tacked lightly with five or six small tacks along each face edge. Temporary tacking is a very important stage in the work of applying fabrics. Very rarely can one position any type of fabric without having to make some slight adjustment in positioning and, by lightly tapping small tacks in the first instance, you can do any necessary repositioning without difficulty. Temporary tacks are easily tapped out and replaced with permanent tacks once the fabric has been found to be positioned satisfactorily.

**1** Antique chair re-covered with floral pattern embroidery on seat and back covering

**2** Bedroom chair covered with gold velvet with deep buttoned back

*Figure 36* Tucking filling under bridle ties

The undercovering stage is important in that it enables the worker to manipulate the filling by tensioning the calico or lining to attain a satisfactory shape and to achieve the amount of doming required. This means that the top covering, which could well be a piece of fine silk or a panel of precious, hand-worked tapestry, will not have to be subjected to any undue strain or run the risk of being damaged through heavy handling.

### Covering

Some ends of the horse-hair filling will undoubtedly project through the undercovering so, to avoid the prickly feeling associated with this type of filling, two or three layers of sheet wadding should be laid over the undercovering material, then trimmed around the top edges. Sides should be free of any filling or wadding to ensure a snug fit into the chair seat rebate.

The first step in applying any patterned covering is to ensure that the positioning of the pattern motifs is right, as a badly positioned motif distracts the eye and will spoil the appearance of the piece.

First, mark centre points on the underside of the seat frame on the front and back members, and also centre mark the reverse side of the covering on the front and back edges. These marks should be aligned when placing the covering. In doing this, take care not to disturb the wadding – do not allow it to fold as, if the covering is a thin material, any fold in the wadding will show through and also, at a later date, the fold line will show as a soil line on the covering.

*Diagram 30* Motif on
covering positioned forward
of centre

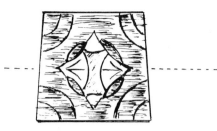

At this stage it should be pointed out that a motif which has a circular
formation should be placed approximately 1.2 to 1.5 cm ($\frac{1}{2}$ to $\frac{5}{8}$ in.) forward
of centre (*diagram 30*). If placed dead centre between the front and back of
the seat, it will appear as if it has been placed too far back when viewed
from a position where one normally would see it. The same would apply to
a back motif; it should be placed 1.2 to 1.5 cm ($\frac{1}{2}$ to $\frac{5}{8}$ in.) higher than centre.

As mentioned earlier, light temporary tacking of the covering is all-
important at the next stage, using five or six 1 or 1.3 cm ($\frac{3}{8}$ or $\frac{1}{2}$ in.) tacks.
The covering should be temporary tacked along the front and back on the
*underside* of the frame aligning centre points and following with each side,
always working from centres to each corner (*diagram 31*). This will ensure
that fullness or loose material is worked into the corners where it can be
dissipated. An exception to the rule of working from centre to corner is
when the side members of a seat are tapered, that is, where the width of the
back of the seat is narrower than the front. In this instance the covering
should be tacked first at the widest point, which would be the front of the
seat on the side member, and then tacked towards the back, at the same
time working loose material to the back corner.

*Diagram 31* System of
temporary tacking and
tensioning of covering

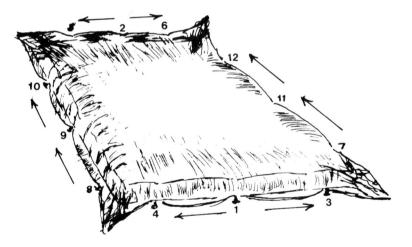

Do not attempt to cut or pleat the corners at the temporary tacking stage
as this should be left until the final tacking.

When satisfied that the covering is positioned and tensioned satisfactorily, again working front and back edges, tap out the temporary tacks one

50

by one as the final tacks are hammered home approximately 1.2 to 1.5 cm ($\frac{1}{2}$ to $\frac{5}{8}$ in.) from the outside edge with spacing of approximately 2.5 to 3 cm (1 to $1\frac{1}{4}$ in.). Generally 1 cm ($\frac{3}{8}$ in.) fine tacks will be suitable for this operation. Diagram 26 (*see page 37*) shows the method of cutting and pleating, covering at the corners, avoiding too much bulk, which would prevent a good fit into the chair rebate. Tack the covering single thickness cutting off the surplus as close to the tacks as possible leaving the edges raw.

To present a neat and tidy finish to the underside of the seat, a lining, preferably black, or even a piece of hessian, should be folded *under* and tacked approximately 1 cm ($\frac{3}{8}$ in.) from the edges of the frame. Spacing of tacks should be approximately 2.5 to 3 cm (1 to $1\frac{1}{4}$ in.).

# Occasional and dining chairs

As with the 'drop-in' seat there are a number of different ways of upholstering a seat intended for occasional or dining chair use, some being screwed to the frame after upholstery and others being upholstered on to the main frame, the latter being more the style of work for period chairs.

## Plywood base

Diagram 32 shows a fairly common and easy method, utilizing a plywood base which, after upholstery, is screwed to the base frame. For re-upholstery of such a seat it is more convenient to remove the seat section from the base frame by undoing the fixing screws and detaching the seat completely.

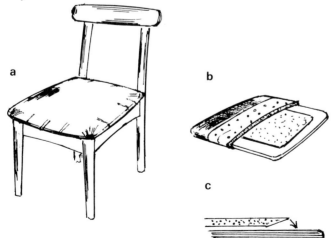

*Diagram 32* (a) popular type of dining chair, (b) section through seat, (c) chamfering of centre foam insert

51

The covering on this type of seat will generally have been fixed on to the plywood by stapling. Fortunately the plywood used for these is soft grain which will allow the staples to be removed reasonably easily. If tacks have been used, these too will present no problem in removal. Under the original covering there probably will have been a sheet of polyether foam 2.5 cm (1 in.) thick but, with deterioration over several years, it may have reduced to powder or at least be flattened. It is therefore wise to be prepared for a shower of powdered foam to fall from the seat when the covering is removed. Any pieces of old foam which may be adhering to the surface of the plywood seat should be removed leaving a clean flat surface for the new layer of foam.

To enhance the appearance and comfort of this thinly upholstered seat, an additional thinner layer of foam of 1.3 cm ($\frac{1}{2}$ in.) thickness, with the edges chamfered, can be laid under the main foam. The cut size of the main foam should be sufficiently large to allow it to overlap the plywood edges so that the perimeter, or outer edge, of the seat is padded. This will give the seat a slightly thicker appearance. (This main foam layer should be 2.5 cm (1 in.) thickness.) The thinner underlay piece of foam should be cut smaller so that it is well short of the sides (*diagram 32c*). Adhesive should be applied to the plywood and around the underside perimeter of the foam, then the two placed together carefully and accurately. For economy, the adhesive need only be applied in a band approximately 5 to 6 cm (2 to $2\frac{1}{2}$ in.) wide around the sides, front and back of the plywood and foam. Contact adhesives recommended for sticking foam are sometimes very fierce so care should be taken to ensure that the foam is not misplaced in the first instance. To try to reposition could mean tearing or damaging the foam.

### Covering

To assess the amount of covering required allow approximately 4 cm ($1\frac{1}{2}$ in.) for fold under at the edges of the seat on the four sides. This type of seat frequently has an overlap of plywood beyond the main base frame members, and allowing a generous fold under will enable you to tack or staple the fabric beyond the overlap of the plywood seat and be within or under the main frame members.

In most instances two seat covers can be cut from a width of upholstery fabric, normally between 122 and 127 cm (48 and 50 in.), that is if the material is placed on the seats with the half width *across* the seat (*diagram 6*).

Using 1.3 cm or 1 cm ($\frac{1}{2}$ or $\frac{3}{8}$ in.) tacks or staples temporary tack the seat material in position starting at the centres front and back, aligning centre marks and working on the same principle as in diagram 31. Tension the covering in the direction of the arrows, smoothing out the fullness and wrinkling of the covering into the corners. In this instance there will be no need to cut the material away to form a pleat because the corners have a fairly large radius which will allow the material to be manipulated easily to dissipate the surplus fullness at the rounded corners. To work the fabric at the corner, first tack fabric in centre of radius of plywood on the underside of the centre, then gradually work small pockets of loose material and tack each side of the centre (similar to frilling or pleating) until all the material is secured. Waste material on the outside of the tacking line should be trimmed away, particularly at the corners, to avoid an uneven or bumpy appearance. The seat should be finished by tacking lining over the base of the seat to present a tidy finish when viewed from the underside. Note the position of the original screw holes so that there will be no difficulty in replacing the seat in its original position.

## Tack-roll seat

A slightly deeper and perhaps more comfortable stuffed upholstered seat for a dining or occasional chair, involving a more traditional approach is shown in diagram 25 and figures 37 and 38. This is a similar method of upholstery as that used for the stool which was described on page 36.

Webbing is applied to the upper edges of the seat frame members using $2 \times 3$ strands of jute or linen webbing or $3 \times 3$ strands for the larger elbow or carver seats.

*Figure 37* Forming the tack-roll

*Figure 38* Completed tack-roll with stitching added to give a sharper and firmer edge

Hessian is then tacked over the webbing, being tensioned whilst being tacked. The top outer edge of the timber frame should be rasped to form a bevel or chamfer if not already done. Then tack the 10 cm (4 in.) wide strip of hessian into position along this chamfer with 1 cm ($\frac{3}{8}$ in.) tacks all around the seat. This can then be infilled to form the tack-roll.

Loose filling or foam is infilled within the tack-roll edge. Ample filling should be used to give the seat a good doming above the tack-roll edge – failure to do this will cause the seat to develop a concave appearance at an early stage in its use. The filling and tack-roll should be covered by a piece of lining or calico as an undercover before the outer covering is tacked into position, the outer covering being placed over two or three layers of sheet wadding to insulate any unevenness in the filling or edges. Figure 39 shows use of tack-roll on an arm facing, and diagram 33 shows the use of a plywood strip on an arm facing to simulate a tack-roll.

In most cases the final covering will be finished on the underside of the seat members unless there is a polished rebate around the face sides in which case the covering should be tacked carefully using small tacks, i.e. 1 cm ($\frac{3}{8}$ in.) fine, avoiding damage to the polished edge of the rebate. A gimp or braid should be used to hide the tacks along the rebate, being stuck with an adhesive, such as 'Copydex', with the gimp being held in place with temporary tacks until the adhesive has set (*figure 40*).

This method of upholstery using the tack-roll simulates the deeply stuffed and stitched type of upholstery found in genuine antique pieces but it does not involve the laborious work of stitching.

54

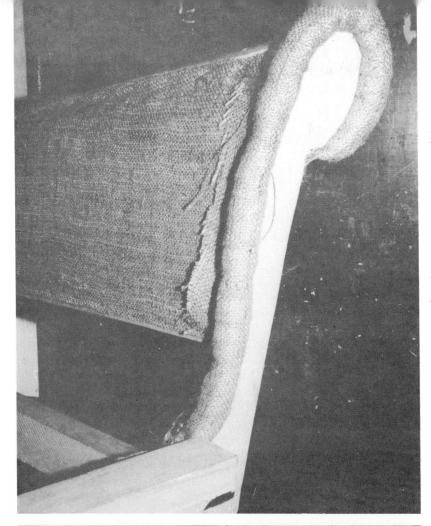

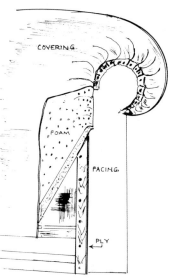

*Diagram 33* Use of plywood strip to imitate tack-roll or stitched edge effect on arm facing

*Figure 39* Tack-roll around arm facing

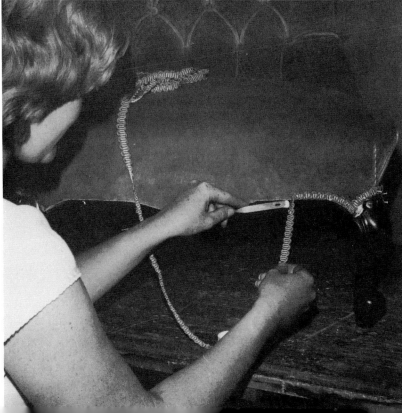

*Figure 40* Sticking gimp to bottom edge of easy chair

# Restoration of antique chairs

A number of readers will, no doubt, be seeking advice on the restoration of upholstery of a valued antique chair and will be desirous of attempting to reproduce the same effect of the fully upholstered seat as the original before deterioration. This involves rather more work than the tack-roll method, using horse-hair filling which, in turn, is encased with upholsterer's scrim, with the edges being stitched into a fine roll using twine and a 20 or 25 cm (8 or 10 in.) long upholsterer's stitching needle (*figure 41*).

Seats of older antique chairs dating back to pre 1825–30 would not have been upholstered with coil springs as these were not used in England until around that time. One often comes across period reproduction chairs which have seats upholstered with some form of springing, either the normal coil springs or the sinuous type of modern springing. For comfortable sitting, of course, the inclusion of springing is an advantage, especially for a dining chair seat on which one often sits for relatively long periods.

Upholstering in the true period style without springing involves 'top' stuffing, that is with the webbing tacked on the top face of the seat members. The base of webbing and hessian should be tacked into position using $3 \times 2$ or $3 \times 3$ strands of webbing with hessian tensioned over, using

*Figure 41* Stuffed and stitched chair seat

1.3 cm ($\frac{1}{2}$ in.) fine tacks. Bridle ties of twine should be sewn into the hessian, as described for the traditional method of working the loose seat, using the same number of loops as the areas to be filled are roughly the same. The bridle ties in this instance need to be a little slacker than for the loose seat because of the extra amount of filling which will be required for the deeper amount of filling.

## Stuffing

Probably the most difficult part of the next stage is using judgement in assessing how much filling to apply under the bridle ties. If re-upholstering the seat you will, no doubt, have previously recorded the original height of the front edge of the seat from the base of the seat frame. The aim is to keep the height the same as the original. Filling around the outside edges will need to be packed in fairly firmly under the bridle ties. Try experimenting by laying the scrim over the filling, then temporary tacking the scrim and making a roll by holding the scrim in position without tacking it fully home, then pressing it with the fingers. This will give some indication as to whether or not the amount of filling will be adequate to give a firm edge. An underfilled edge will concertina when under compression during sitting and will not return to the original height.

Scrim temporary tacked over the filling should not be tensioned tightly but left slack. Twine ties should now be sewn through the scrim from above, through the filling and out through the base hessian and webbing, returning through the webbing and hessian approximately 1 to 1.2 cm ($\frac{3}{8}$ to $\frac{1}{2}$ in.) further along the weave. For a seat such as this you will need three ties along each direction in a running line from first position to last, the first and last ties being the only ones to be knotted after the twine has been tightened between all the ties. The twine connecting all the ties should be seen to run parallel with the weave of the scrim as near as possible, as shown in figure 41.

Centre temporary tacks holding the scrim along the front face of the seat may now be tapped out to enable the scrim to be folded *under* and finally tacked home neatly, with the fold following the weave, using 1 cm ($\frac{3}{8}$ in.) tacks along the bevelled edge on the top edge of the seat rail member. Tacks should be hammered home with the heads lying flat and spaced evenly along the bevel with approximately 1 to 1.3 cm ($\frac{3}{8}$ to $\frac{1}{2}$ in.) spacing. At the beginning this stage is rather critical so should be given some attention, as the first tacks will govern the finished height of the stitched seat edge. Also, whilst the scrim is being folded under and progressively tacked, any loose projecting strands of yarn or filling should be tucked in. This is easily accomplished using the flat end of the upholsterer's regulator.

## Stitching

With the tacking down of the scrim completed on all four sides of the seat, stitching may be started. Three types of stitching are frequently required but not always necessary, depending upon the height of the edge being worked. The first stage is to put in 'blind' stitching. This is a series of stitches which form loops of twine within the scrim and filling – they do not appear on the surface of the scrim (*diagram 34*). When eased tight progressively after each stitch they will draw the filling towards the edge to consolidate the edge filling ready for the next stage of stitching.

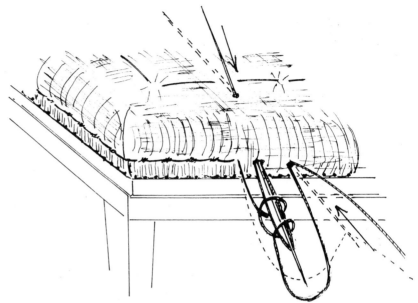

*Diagram 34* Forming the blind stitch

Diagrams 27 and 35 (*see page 38*) show seats with different depths of upholstery. Diagram 27, thinnest of the two seats, will require two rows of stitching only, e.g. 'blind' stitch and fine 'top' stitch. In diagram 35 the seat is deeper with a consequent higher edge and this will require an additional row of stitching to reinforce the increased depth of filling, e.g. 'blind' stitch, 'thumb roll' stitch, and fine 'top' stitch.

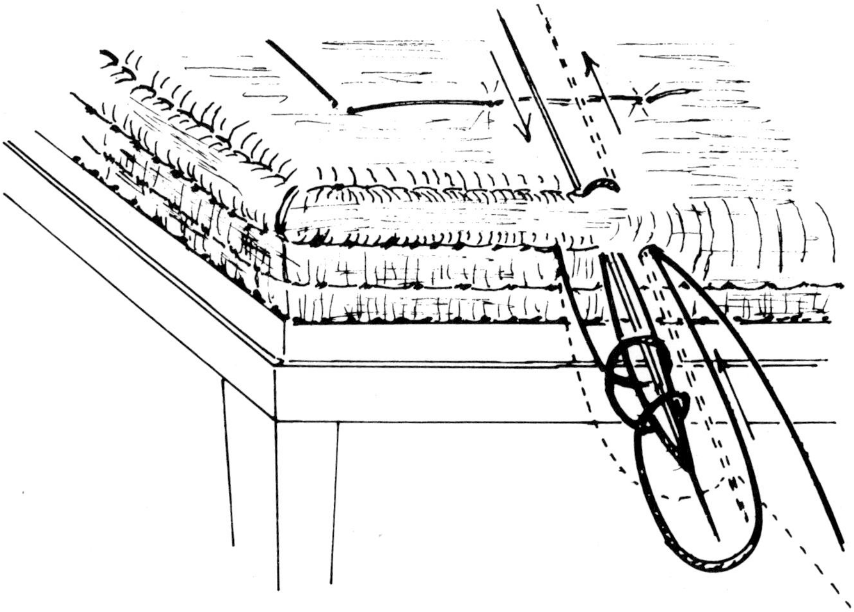

*Diagram 35* Forming the roll stitch; the 'fine' top stitch is formed by the same method

Diagrams 34 and 35 show how these stitches are formed using good quality upholsterer's flax twine and a 20 to 25 cm (8 to 10 in.) upholsterer's long stitching needle, the blind and roll stitches being worked preferably with a bayonet needle and the top stitch with a fine needle, although either will do the work in an emergency.

Whilst progressing around the edge forming the stitch, the upholsterer's regulator should be used to 'regulate' the filling (*diagram 36*): move uneven filling by penetrating the scrim with the point of the regulator and with a deft twist of the wrist shift the filling as required to even it along the edge. This operation will not damage the scrim and any holes made in the loose weave will tend to close whilst handling and stitching. Normal working for stitching is from left to right.

*Diagram 36* Regulating filling

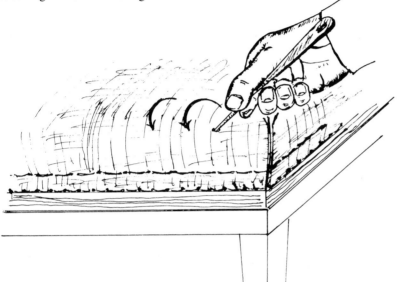

After completing the blind stitch, put in the intermediate roll stitch if it is necessary. To form it, the needle should enter the scrim on the face edge approximately 1.3 cm ($\frac{1}{2}$ in.) above the line of the blind stitch, being careful to keep to this line on all sides without deviating. The roll stitch, unlike the blind stitch, should appear on the top surface of the scrim, i.e. the needle and twine should be drawn out through the upper surface and re-enter some 1.2 to 1.3 cm ($\frac{1}{2}$ in.) back towards the previous stitch. A series of continuous stitches, without gaps between, should appear at the top side of the roll.

To attain a 'sharp' edge to the seat a fine top stitch should now be sewn in. This is a similar operation to working the roll stitch but is smaller, approximately the thickness of your little finger, the filling and scrim being pinched with the fingers of the left hand as the twine is pulled tight with the other hand. If done correctly, this should have the effect of producing flat stitching which should protrude slightly in an upwards direction to counter the pull of material strained over it. When applying filling after the stitching is completed, it should lie within the stitched line and not protrude over the edge as this would detract from the stitch sharpness.

## Second stuffing

Bridle ties should now be sewn into the scrim in the same way as earlier into the hessian. In this instance, the twine loops should be a little tighter as a smaller amount of filling is to be tucked under them (*see figure 41 on page 56*).

The second stuffing of a high quality chair seat would normally have been of horse hair, if stuffed in the traditional manner. In re-using this, it will need 'teasing' – that is, pulling the long hair strands apart with the fingers to re-introduce the original resilience of new, curled hair. Invariably this is very dusty work and it is advisable to wear some form of mask and do it in the open air to avoid inhaling the fine dust emanating from the hair.

The loosely teased filling should be applied less densely around the edges but built up rather more boldly towards the centre (but not overdone) to give the domed effect.

## Undercover

With the filling distributed satisfactorily, apply the undercover of linen or calico, tacking on the face edges of front, back and side members, temporary tacking beforehand. When tacking the undercovering home, using pressure from the fingers, mould any irregularities in the stitched edge through the fabric of the undercover, into smooth, even lines.

Two or three layers of sheet wadding (depending upon the quality) are needed over the undercover to avoid strands of loose horse hair working through the outer covering. The wadding should be laid over the upper surface and down the sides, being trimmed short of the base edges.

## Covering

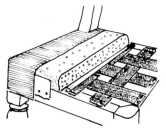

*Diagram 37* Dining chair with deep foam filling

Covering should be laid over the wadding without disturbing or causing a fold. Ensure the weave of the covering is lying straight and square with the back, front and sides of the seat. The next step is to complete temporary tacking of the covering into position on the underside of the seat members. Check the position of motif or stripes by standing the chair on the floor and overlooking, as any fault should be corrected at this stage whilst still temporary tacked. Finally, tack home using 1 cm ($\frac{3}{8}$ in.) tacks on the underside, finishing with a bottoming of linen, calico or hessian neatly folded under to cover the raw edges.

*Diagram 38* Feeling the rebate edge with the tip of the thumb, using the thumb nail to guide the hammer on to the tack head to avoid damaging the polished finish under the loose covering

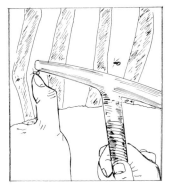

# Pouffes

Pouffes have always been a popular item of upholstered furniture, particularly during the winter months as an easy, informal seat by the fire.

There are probably as many styles of floor pouffes as there are styles of upholstered suites. Pouffes are a popular item for the beginner of home upholstery to undertake, probably because of the manageable size and apparent lack of complication, and the fact that materials are relatively easy and inexpensive to obtain. A pouffe is also a suitable vehicle on which to use some hand-woven or hand-worked panel.

## Traditional pouffe

The older style of pouffe (*diagram 39*) is formed from a circular bag or case which is machined to the required size and filled with some form of loose filling. Wood-wool (fine strands of wood) is usually used for this purpose and is packed very tightly into the case through a small opening which is then sewn up. An ornamental upholstery cord is usually pulled tightly around the centre to give it the 'cottage loaf' appearance. Wood-wool is generally easily obtainable free of cost from a local china or pottery store as it is used as packing material and is usually discarded after the contents of the packing cases have been emptied.

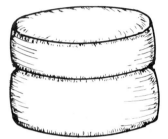

*Diagram 39* Circular pouffe

When using the wood-wool as a filling, it should be packed into the pouffe case as tightly and firmly as possible. Loose packing allows movement of the fine strands of wood which will fracture repeatedly smaller and smaller until the strands become particles or wood dust.

It is wise to make up an interior case to contain the filling with a separate one made from the outer covering. The outer case can be made up without the base. It can then be easily drawn over the inner, filled case, pinned in position and sewn around the bottom edges of the inner case. A base can then be attached, preferably using P.V.C. as this will allow the pouffe to be slid around carpeting easily. It will also minimize wear and soiling.

## Dual-purpose pouffe

A dual-purpose pouffe is shown in diagram 40. This is a box pouffe which has an amount of storage space within the box section below a deep upholstered seat section filled with foam.

Whilst diagram 40 shows a base of simple construction utilizing prefabricated board (chipboard or particle board) of minimum 1.3 cm ($\frac{1}{2}$ in.) thickness, it is possible to utilize an existing box of suitable size and sound construction.

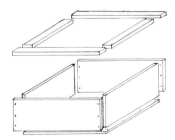

*Diagram 40* Exploded view of square box pouffe construction

The inside of the box should be upholstered first being lightly padded thinly with one or two thicknesses of sheet wadding which, in turn, is covered with a suitable colour lining to match the outer covering. For appearance sake the inside of the box should be as neatly and carefully upholstered as the exterior.

With the base panel of the box removed, cover two opposite sides with the wadding and lining, cutting the wadding tight up to the corner but leaving sufficient surplus lining to overlap around the corner to enable the lining from the adjacent side to be folded under right into the corner without showing a break. The fold down the corner should be slip-stitched neatly (*diagram 5*). This is more convenient to attempt before the base and top are fixed in position, but after the lining has been tacked to the top and bottom edges of the side members using small tacks, i.e. 1 cm ($\frac{3}{8}$ in.) fine.

The lining for the base should at this stage be tensioned across the open bottom and tacked into position again on the edges of the side members, over the tacking position of the inside lining. This should be tacked single thickness, not folded. Lay one or two layers of sheet wadding over this base lining, then place the base board into position. It may be necessary to square up the sides to line up with the edges of the base board, as the edges of the base *must* be flush with the outside lines of the sides. The base board is either screwed in position, having been previously drilled to accept the screws, or fixed with slender nails 3 to 3.6 cm ($1\frac{1}{4}$ to $1\frac{1}{2}$ in.) long. This should give the appearance shown in figure 42, which also shows clearly the outer covering fixed along the top edges of the sides of the box, the edge of the covering being lined up with the inner edge of the sides. Diagram 41 shows how the covering is fixed in position by the 'back-tacking' method.

*Figure 42* Lined interior of box pouffe

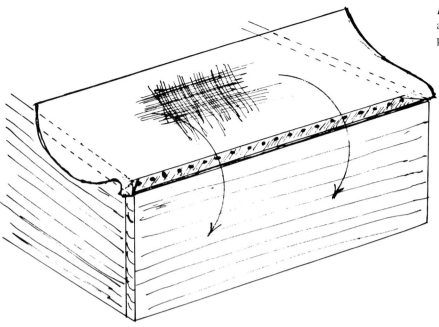

*Diagram 41* Back-tacking
along top edge of sides of box
pouffe

## Back-tacking

Back-tacking is a simple method of fixing covering so that the line of tacks
holding it is hidden, and it may be used in a number of situations requiring
the fixing of fabric on seat borders, outside backs, outside arms, etc.
(*diagram 42*). For the back-tacking of covering on the edges of the box, cut
four strips of stout card using a rule and sharp knife to ensure straight
edges. These strips should be cut to the same width as the sides of the box.

*Diagram 42* Back-tacking
along face of seat borders,
outside arms, etc.

FACE SIDE OF
COVERING.

REVERSE SIDE OF
COVERING.

Using small tacks (i.e. 1 cm [$\frac{3}{8}$ in.] fine) tack the outer covering with just three or four tacks along the top edge of the side to hold it into place before using the strip of card, keeping the material tensioned lightly along its length. At this stage the material should be lying into the centre of the box with wrong side uppermost. When satisfied the covering is in the correct position, tack the card along the edge covering the edge of material and the few tacks holding it. The tacking should be quite close, approximately 1 cm ($\frac{3}{8}$ in.), to give a flat surface, and tacking any wider apart will give a series of humps showing where tacks have been placed. Corner joins should be mitred.

Lay sufficient wadding over the outer surface of the box side to give the depth of padding required, not taking it over the top edge. One layer of wadding will suffice over the back-tacking card. Carefully, without disturbing or folding the wadding, bring the covering down and tack on the underside of the base. Again work opposite sides, tacking the ends of the first two sides round the corners. After back-tacking the remaining two sides and padding to the same depth as the previous sides, tack along the base and, in the first instance, pin along the depth of the corners, smoothing any looseness into the pinned line. The join down the corners should be slip-stitched as the inside corners.

### Upholstery of lid top

The upper part of the box pouffe which forms the lid is upholstered on a base board of the same thickness as the sides. Before starting the upholstery, the position of the hinges should be ascertained and holes drilled at the screw positions. Good quality brass hinges should be selected for this as there is considerable strain on hinges in this situation.

*Diagram 43* (a) butting edges of covering at corner, the hatched areas to be cut away, (b) folds of covering butted together and slip-stitched

**a**

**b**

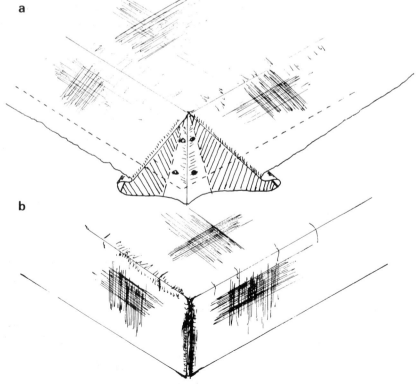

Interior foam for the lid section should be 7.5 or 10 cm (3 or 4 in.) in thickness and of firm density. It should be cut 6 mm ($\frac{1}{4}$ in.) oversize all round and be held in position with adhesive applied to the surface of the foam and board.

A simple method of covering the lid section is by the wrap method – that is laying the covering across the top surface and allowing it to drape down the sides to be tacked or stapled to the underside of the board. Treatment of corners is as in diagram 43a and b, by cutting the surplus covering away, then folding, butting the folded corners together and, finally, slip-stitching the folds together. The base of the lid section should be covered with the matching lining as used for the interior of the box.

## Framed lid

An alternative method of constructing the upper lid or seat section is shown in diagram 40. This is utilizing a framed construction with timber (beech) members of minimum size of 5 × 2.3 cm (2 × $\frac{7}{8}$ in.), put together with dowelled joints. Using an open frame such as this, will allow the use of resilient rubber webbing on the upper or top surface of the frame, thus giving a deeper sprung effect. For a frame of, say, 46 to 50 cm (18 to 20 in.) square, four strands should be used one way with one or two only in the other direction. Figure 43 shows a box pouffe covered with P.V.C., with a 'float' buttoned lid.

Figure 43 Box pouffe covered in P.V.C. with buttoned lid

Interior foam in this instance should be fixed in position by sticking strips of cotton calico or linen around the sides of the foam so that a flange is left at the bottom edge, this then being stapled or tacked to the outer edge of the frame. Covering of the framed top may be carried out in the same way as the boarded base.

A more attractive finish can be given to the upholstery of the lid section by using piping or ruching around the top edge between the top panel and side borders. You will need to use a sewing machine capable of working thicker than normal domestic work. The width of fabric to be cut to form the piping should be cut on the bias (*diagram 44a*) 3.6 cm ($1\frac{1}{2}$ in.) wide, being made up using a pre-shrunk soft piping cord.

Cutting the top panel should be undertaken with care, cutting the fabric square with the weave of the cloth and leaving an extra 1 cm ($\frac{3}{8}$ in.) for seaming and, if necessary, trimming the flange of the made-up piping to the same width. The same seaming allowance should be given on the fabric if ruche is to be used. When fitting the piped or ruched top on to the foam, ensure that the flange or seam is lying down the sides, i.e. against the borders, and not on the top surface of the foam (*diagram 44b*).

*Diagram 44* (a) cutting of fabric for bias piping, (b) flange of piping positioned down side of border

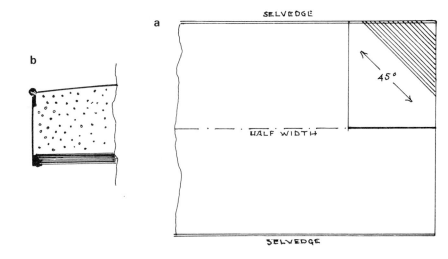

## Kidney-shaped pouffe

A kidney-shaped box pouffe trimmed with ruche is shown in figures 44 and 45 and colour plate 4. This is a more ambitious project than the square or rectangular shape. The kidney shaping of this pouffe is formed on the outside edges of the timber, framed-up members – the inner lines being square to form the interior box. It will be noted that ruche is tacked around the base of the top section in addition to the upper edge. This will camouflage the break between top and bottom sections.

*Figure 44* Kidney-shaped box
pouffe trimmed with ruche
and fringe

*Figure 45* Kidney-shaped box
pouffe with raised lid showing
lined interior

# Replacing springing and webbing

## Coil springing

Coil springing (i.e. the waisted or hour-glass type of spring) has over recent years been ousted by a number of other, more modern methods of springing, most of which allow for the more slender upholstered line demanded by the contemporary designer and his customer.

However, coil spring *units* do still have a place in mass production and are frequently used where a deeply upholstered seat or back is desired. These single-framed units are joined together and attached to the chair or settee frame in a single operation more speedily than the individual coil springs used to be (*figure 46*).

Unfortunately, the occasional fault will occur with these spring units: one spring may fracture, giving off a metallic grinding noise when sat upon, or a spring may become crippled through misuse, or perhaps with constant use and a bad sitter's posture it may become weak on one side of a seat. Troubles such as these are very difficult for the D.I.Y. home upholsterer to rectify as replacement units would be practically impossible to obtain. The best advice is to discard the faulty unit and to re-upholster the seat using linen webbing and separate coil springs.

Hand-made, custom-built upholstery work, which is by no means dead these days, frequently calls for the use of the waisted coil spring, together with the use of traditional methods of upholstery filling and style of work. Also in the restoration of period pieces and the carrying out of period reproduction work, the use of the coil spring is very much in evidence. I feel it is worth recording this process within these chapters.

The double cone spring (its technical name) is available in a range of sizes (depending upon the supplier's stocks), from 7.5 cm (3 in.) to 36 cm (14 in.). They are also made in different gauges (thicknesses of wire) which, of course, has an effect upon the strength or resistance of the spring against compression when sat upon.

### Spring gauges

The gauges of wire from which upholstery springs are made vary from 8 S.W.G. (standard wire gauge), the stoutest, which makes a very firm spring, to 15 S.W.G., being the lightest type of spring. For seating purposes, the thicker gauges should be used, say 8 to 10 gauge – 8 gauge making a very firm seat, 9 gauge being average and 10 gauge giving quite a soft result. For back or arm springing, the lighter gauges of 11 or 12 S.W.G. should be used. The lightest, 15 S.W.G., is normally used for the spring units of sprung mattresses.

## Webbing

When coil springing is to be introduced into seat upholstery the supporting linen or jute webbing should be tacked on to the *underside* of the seat framework, the tacks being positioned as in diagram 45, with five tacks on the folded ends (the first ends to be tacked), three tacks on the single layer of webbing being tensioned and a further two on the fold after cutting. Do not pre-cut the strands to length as this makes for difficult tensioning and is wasteful. It is better to work from the roll.

*Figure 46* Showing a back spring unit with single cone coil springs

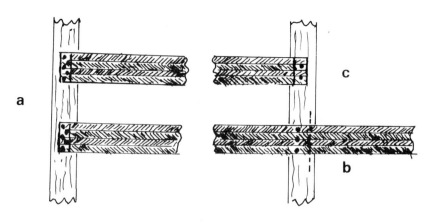

*Diagram 45* Method of tacking linen or jute woven webbing: (a) stage 1, using five tacks, (b) stage 2, three tacks after tensioning, (c) stage 3, fold over with two tacks on fold between the three underneath

a

c

b

### Sewing in springs

Ample strands of webbing should be used to support the base coil of the spring. Webbing should be arranged so that as much of the base of the spring is supported as possible. Figure 47 shows the underside of the sprung dining chair seat with 3 × 3 strands of webbing supporting 9 springs 12.5 cm (5 in.) high and 10 S.W.G. This springing would be suitable for the stuffed seat shown in figure 41 (*see page 56*). It will be noted that the springs are sited on the cross-over of the strands of web. Also the illustration shows each spring base has four ties around the circle, each tie being knotted before the twine continues to the next tie point. Sewing-in of the springs is done from the underside of the webbing using a spring (curved) needle and flax twine. As the needle emerges through the base, turn the twine around it and then withdraw it to form a single knot. It is often the practice of professional upholsterers to secure each spring with three ties only.

*Figure 47* Crossed webbing supporting coil springs

## Lashing

Springs should not be positioned too closely to the front, back and side members of the frame because after the bases of the springs are sewn, the top coils should be lashed in both directions with laidcord (thick flax or hemp cord) to prevent any lateral movement. Also, the outer rows should be canted slightly away from the centre of the seat (*figure 48*). As shown here four knots are necessary on the top coil to hold the spring securely in position. How to form the clove-hitch knot is shown in diagram 46.

*Diagram 46* Forming the clove-hitch knot

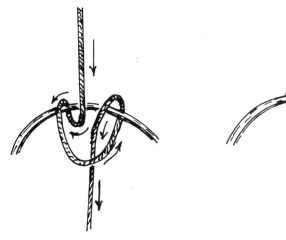

*Figure 48* Method of lashing springs in an easy chair seat

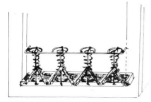

*Diagram 47* Construction of spring edge on easy chair seat

*Figure 49* Springing of easy chair back with coil springs

### Easy chair seat springing

Figure 48, shows an easy chair seat being worked, with nine springs sewn in the 'well' of the seat and lashed into position. The side and back rows of springs are set so that there is a clearance between them and the bottom of the arms and back to allow filling to be tucked easily down the sides and back of the seat after the hessian has been applied. This figure also shows the front edge springs being lashed into position after being fixed to the front rails using wire 'U' staples 1.3 cm ($\frac{1}{2}$ in.) in length. These springs will give the seat the highly desirable spring edge and make a very comfortable seat.

After stapling, a strand of webbing should be tacked over the base coil to prevent any possible 'chattering' or noise caused by the lower coils of the spring contacting the wood and any tacks. Diagram 47 shows the complete lashing of the front edge springs and the fixing of the edge cane or wire (whichever has been selected). This gives the unbroken straight line to the top of the edge springs.

### Back springing

Figure 49 shows springs set in the back of a wing easy chair. 4 × 4 strands of webbing are tacked on the outside of the top and side members. It will be noticed that the webbing on the back stay rail (the intermediate rail) is tacked on the inner face and not on the outside as is the remainder – this has the effect of bringing forward the bottom line of the inside back which is sometimes desirable.

72

**3** Attaching covered upholstery buttons to arm of leather easy chair

**4** Kidney-shaped box pouffe with ruche and fringe trimming

**5** Foot stool with embroidered floral pattern covering trimmed with fringe

**6** Elbow (or carver) chair
with 'drop-in' loose seat
covered with leather

The gauge of spring being used here is 12 S.W.G. (a light spring), being lashed into position using a stout flax twine instead of the heavier cord used for seats. This helps to preserve the resilience of the lightly sprung and stuffed upholstery of the back. When lashing back springs they should be given a light upwards tilt and lashed in that position to counteract the downwards drag of the back as a person sits in the chair.

*Figure 50* Fixing of springs on to arm rail

### *Arm springing*

Fixing springing in position for a sprung arm is shown in figure 50. Again, very light springs should be used but these do become damaged if the arm is sat upon – a habit of which, unfortunately, a number of people are guilty.

## Rubber webbing – an alternative method of suspension

An easy chair with seat and back springing exposed stripped of the old upholstery is shown ready to be re-upholstered in figure 46 (*see page 69*). The springing of the seat, now unserviceable, was with nine tension springs. One spring is unaccountably missing, as is so often the case, and others are over-stretched, with the plastic sleeving broken away in a number of places.

The whole seat springing is very unsightly which is all the more important as this form of springing is normally left open to view when the seat cushion is lifted.

It would be difficult for the average D.I.Y. home upholsterer to obtain a replacement supply of these springs unless within reasonable distance of a good all-round supplier. As an alternative method of seat suspension rubber webbing could be considered. Like foam, rubber webbing greatly simplifies home upholstery. With characteristics similar to a flat spring, and used in conjunction with a foam cushion, it will frequently obviate the need for the deeper kind of coil spring and traditional stuffing. A quick, easy-to-fit, relatively cheap example is Pirelli resilient rubber webbing which should be tacked across the seat in the same direction as the springs were fitted. The ends are easily hidden under a panel of covering to match the cushion (*diagram 48*). The original tension springs were held in position by being hooked through holes in two long metal plates screwed along each side of the seat. The plates were held with four or five screws into the timber of the side seat rails. Unhook the springs and unscrew the plates – both plates and springs may be discarded (*diagram 49*).

*Diagram 48* Tacked ends of rubber webbing covered with side panels of covering

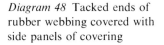

*Diagram 49* Anchorage of tension springing showing fixing plates screwed to frame

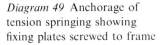

### Tensioning rubber webbing

Six strands of standard Pirelli rubber webbing 5 cm (2 in.) wide are needed to replace the tension springs. These will give better support for the cushions because the webbing is much wider than the original springs, leaving narrower spaces between for the cushion to be forced into. The six strands of webbing should be tensioned *across* the seat only at a tension of approximately 7.5 to 10 per cent – so that if the width across the seat is, say, 50 cm ($19\frac{1}{2}$ in.), the stretch given to the rubber webbing should be approximately 3.75 to 5 cm ($1\frac{1}{2}$ to 2 in.).

Do not cut the strands of rubber webbing off individually. Work out the positions for the webbing and mark prior to tacking, working from the roll, tack one end using four or five tacks (only 1.3 cm [$\frac{1}{2}$ in.] fine tacks); do not fold over as woven webbing but tack on the single thickness. Rubber webbing will not fray like the woven type.

Having assessed the amount of tension the webbing is to be given, mark with a pencil or biro where the inner frame touches the webbing across the other side of the seat. Then, again, mark off the amount of tension from the first mark towards the centre, and the space between these two marks is the amount the webbing needs to move to give the desired tension. By working to this method on each strand, each will have its correct amount of stretch and each will have the same deflection.

Rubber webbing is not normally applied in both directions nor is it interlaced. Strands in one direction only will suffice for normal applications. One exception to this is where webbing is being applied to a curved 'spoon' back where cross-webbing is necessary to retain the hollow shape of the back (*diagram 50*).

When applying rubber webbing to a settee or couch seat the strands of webbing should be tacked in position from back to front instead of from side to side. Because of the additional length, the webbing would have too much deflection and sag overmuch. It is unnecessary to use any type of webbing stretcher when working with rubber webbing as suitable tensions can usually be obtained by hand.

The back spring unit exposed in figure 46 (*see page 69*) is in sound condition and re-usable, as is usually the case. Due to the light loading to which a chair or settee back is subjected, it is generally safe to assume that the springs can be re-used. A wise precaution whilst the back spring unit is in its open state is to tie cords from the front bottom wire frame at each point where the coil springs are attached to the wire mesh top (three), then passing each cord through the springs without tying, and fixing on to the top back rail with a large tack. The object of this operation is to ensure that the springs are held at an angle slightly in an upwards direction, in line with pressure of the body downwards when a person sits. This also applies to hand springing of a back as described earlier. Re-upholstery of this chair is described in a later chapter.

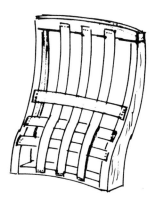

*Diagram 50* Method of application of rubber webbing to a shaped back.

### Attaching rubber webbing

There are several useful and simple ways of attaching rubber webbing,

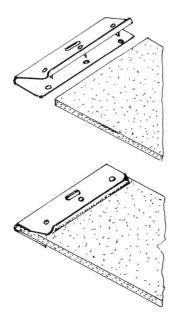

*Diagram 51* Fixing of steel clips to rubber webbing

some suitable for fixing it to timber framework and others for attaching it to steel or tubular constructions.

In some instances, existing rubber webbing may have become unserviceable through deterioration or abrasion against part of the frame. On examination, it may be found that the strands of webbing are held in position in a slot along the side member of the seat by means of a pressed steel clip attached to the ends of each strand of webbing instead of being tacked.

It is wise to assume that all the strands of webbing will be roughly in the same condition so all should be replaced. Replacement Pirelli rubber webbing may be purchased at most local D.I.Y. stores and the same stores will usually stock the steel clips (*diagram 51*). These are supplied in the open state ready for slipping the webbing into the jaws.

When fitting the ends of the strands into the clips, the use of a bench vice is required to ensure that the jaws of the clips close tightly on to the webbing. Before clamping, make sure that the clips on each strand end are both the same way round. There is a short flange on one face of the clip which must fit adjacent to the groove edge (*diagram 51*).

In assessing the length of strands to fit between the grooves, measure straight across between the grooves, deduct the amount of tension or stretch to be given ($7\frac{1}{2}$ to 10 per cent), then add 1.3 cm ($\frac{1}{2}$ in.) each end for the slotting of the clip into the groove. The clip must be clamped up as tightly as possible so that the prongs of the clips penetrate through the rubber webbing to prevent any slippage. It is a simple matter to fit the clip into the slot one side and stretch the webbing across to allow the second clip to slot in, the flange of the clip being on the underside.

# Stile and collar cutting

### Stile cutting

The problem of 'stile cutting', i.e. cutting upholstery materials to fig snugly around an obstructing rail or post, often proves a major obstacle for many home upholsterers. Making cuts into perhaps expensive top covering, of course, needs to be undertaken carefully and precisely. Due to the importance of this operation, and the obvious tell-tale traces if badly done, it is usually attempted by the amateur with some trepidation.

## Confidence and a good pair of scissors

Good cutting in any form is usually the result of confidence and the use of foresight, planning and, of course, a good sharp pair of scissors, particularly at the points which are mostly used for the cutting of stiles. Generally a good pair of scissors made from good steel will retain their sharpness over a number of years. If a fault develops it could be one of two things – either the rivet or small nut and bolt holding the blades together will have worked slack and will need attention to draw the blades tighter together, or the cutting edges of the blades may need honing with a few rubs with a carborundum stone.

Honing the blades is a simple job done in a few moments and well worth the time taken as a blunt pair of scissors will prove very frustrating and result in jagged cuts. When rubbing the carborundum stone along the blades use the fine side of the stone and ensure the existing cutting edge angle is maintained. A few rubs every so often will keep a pair of scissors keen for cutting all types of coverings and materials.

Unfortunately stiles are a necessary evil in upholstery frame making, as it is impossible to construct a chair or settee frame with continuous free clearance around the sides and back to allow the interior materials and top covering to be taken from the inside of the frame through to the outside tacking line.

There are a number of different types of stiles in upholstery work which have to be cut around, each needing a different approach. Some typical stiles are illustrated here with the appropriate method of cutting shown (*diagrams 52 and 53*). It is very important, before any cutting of the stile is attempted, that the covering or other material being worked is correctly placed, i.e. centred, with a suitable amount of working material on each of the four sides for tacking purposes. This applies whether it be an inner material or the final covering. Also, equally important, make sure that the weave of the material is straight and square with the sides of the frame. Remember that once the material has been cut wrongly the error is irreversible. It will be found from experience that cutting stiles off the straight weave will cause difficulty in getting the material to set and pleat at corners correctly.

**a**

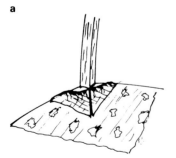

**b**

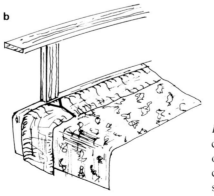

*Diagram 52* (a) cutting covering around corner stile of dining chair seat, (b) cutting covering around arm stile of fireside chair

*Diagram 53* Cutting covering
around different stiles on a
'tub' chair seat

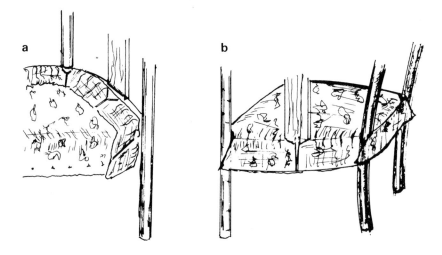

## Collar cutting

A similar problem to that of stile cutting on a bigger scale but not so
frequently necessary. A collar is a strip of covering material sewn to each
side of the inside back where it fits adjacent to the arms (*diagram 54*). The
back covering is tailored by snipping and cutting carefully around the
shaped arm with the collar then being machined along the curved cut each
side of the back. This operation ensures that when the back is fitted it will
lay unwrinkled and clean around the shaped arm. If a collar is not fitted
with a scroll shaped arm, such as illustrated, the back will need over-cutting
to remove wrinkling and fullness with the disadvantage that the cuts will be
readily felt by the fingers just inside the joining line of back and arm.
Frequently with this situation the inner filling may start to protrude after a
period of not-too-careful use.

This process may also be carried out if a square bordered arm is being
dealt with. It can also be used to advantage on an awkward or large stile on
a seat.

*Diagram 54* Cutting back
covering and fitting 'collar'
around shaped arm

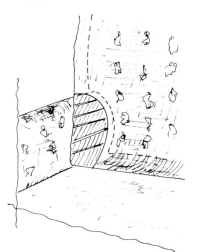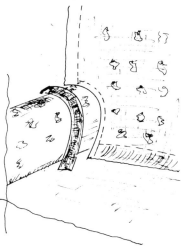

# Planning and cutting covering material

The purchase of covering material for an upholstery project such as an easy chair or settee is usually the heaviest outlay of all the materials to be used. It can prove to be a very costly error if insufficient thought or planning is given to the amount of covering material required. Material may be over-estimated, making the work unnecessarily expensive. Conversely, if under-estimated, it is not always possible to obtain a further small quantity of identical material at a later date to finish the job.

For the best appearance of the cloth on the work it should always be used with the weave, nap or pattern lying in one direction. Varying the direction of the pattern or lines of the weave to suit the economics of cutting will, more often than not, spoil the appearance of the work and even a plain weave cloth will frequently shade differently if laid in different directions.

## Estimating covering

Width of fabric intended for upholstery work is generally 122 to 127 cm (48 to 50 in.). Some high-quality velvet and cretonnes may be 68.5 cm (27 in.) or 91.5 cm (36 in.) wide and other fabrics made from man-made fibres can be up to 137 cm (54 in.) wide.

To avoid over- or under-estimating the quantity of covering needed for an upholstered job, it is advisable to take measurements of the various parts of the covering and plan out on paper the most advantageous and economical method of cutting. Any old covering stripped off can be used as templates by laying the parts out on the floor, side by side, to see which will come out of the width of fabric, and then assessing the length of covering required. This should be done prior to the purchase of the covering. After purchase, the sizes to be cut should be drawn on the reverse side of the material using tailor's chalk. In this way it can be clearly seen if there is sufficient covering or not for the work. After cutting off each piece, write on the reverse side for which part of the work the covering is intended. If this is not done, it is very easy to get the pieces confused.

## Half width

As mentioned earlier, the half-width size of the material is suitable for certain parts of the work. This enables 'pairs' of parts to be cut from the width, e.g. pairs of arms, pairs of outside arms, inside and outside backs, top and bottom panels of cushions, etc. (*diagram 55*).

*Diagram 55* Cutting plan showing use of half widths of covering

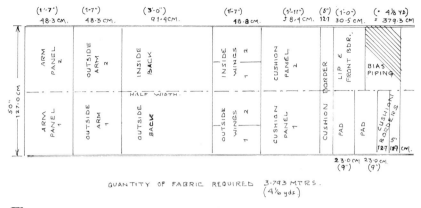

QUANTITY OF FABRIC REQUIRED  3.793 MTRS.
(4⅙ yds)

## Flys

Frequently, to assist in the cutting of pairs of parts and for the sake of economic cutting, 'flys' can be used (*diagram 56*). These are extension strips of material, such as hessian, lining or any form of material cheaper than the covering, which are machined on to the part so that the extension pieces are beyond the sight line when in position on the work and are sufficiently wide to be used for tacking the part in position. The use of flys will save on the total amount of covering needed.

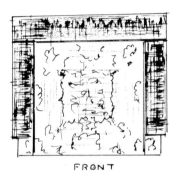

FRONT

*Diagram 56* Use of 'flys' on seat covering

## Platform lining

A further economy in the use of covering is the use of 'platform' lining under seat cushions (*diagram 57*). The lip or front of the seat, approximately 12.5 cm (5 in.) back from the front edge of a stuffed seat, is covered with the actual covering, while the remaining area is covered in a matching lining and the line between the two, formed by the joining seam, is held down by being sewn through the seat using twine and a long needle. Diagrams 55 and 75 show cover plans for the chairs illustrated as examples.

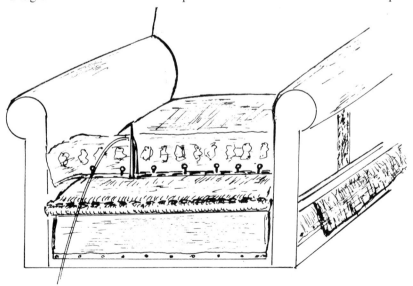

*Diagram 57* Sewing down join between platform seat lining and front lip covering

# Buttoning

Upholstery with buttoning in some form is an ever-popular furnishing fashion. For the D.I.Y. home upholsterer it brings a degree of satisfaction in accomplishing a tricky job. Whilst the original purpose of buttoning was to assist in preserving the shape of curved upholstery and to retain the filling in position, it is now mainly used as a decorative feature of the upholstery design or style.

As fairly expensive dyes, moulds and presses are required for the making of covered upholstery buttons, it is necessary for the home worker to have the buttons made to order, usually by the local departmental or soft-furnishing store supplying your own material. Various sizes of covered buttons are obtainable.

There is a proprietary brand of metal button shell sold on a card called 'Trims' and these are very easy to make up into covered buttons for upholstery use provided the fabric to be used is not too thick. This type of home-made button is fairly successful but will not take too much strain on the wire loop and it is sometimes necessary to pull down tightly on the button when tying off (*diagram 58*).

*Diagram 58* Patented type of D.I.Y. self-make button 'trims'

## Float buttoning

Float buttoning, the simplest form of buttoning (*diagram 59*), may be all that is required for practical purposes in some instances with thinly stuffed upholstery. This method of buttoning leaves the covering without the definite pleating lines between the buttons as found with 'deep' buttoning.

For float buttoning the covering is left slightly slack. By inserting the twine holding the button through the upholstery and pulling down the button, then tacking or tying off at the base or back, the covering tightens, with slight wrinkle lines radiating from the buttons. This type of buttoning finish is used for squab cushions, thinly upholstered work, headboards, etc.

*Diagram 59* Example of float buttoning on shaped seat

## Deep buttoning

The effect of deep buttoning can only be attained when the upholstery filling is of reasonable depth, i.e. a minimum depth of 5 cm (2 in.), although this will not give such good results as deeper filling. The deep buttoned effect can be made, of course, with the normal traditional fillings, such as coir fibre and horse hair, or it can be attained with the modern foam filling latex or polyurethane. If using sheet polyether foam it is advisable to punch holes through the foam at the button positions to enable the button and the covering to sink into the foam rather than have the button pull the foam down to the base. To make a hole approximately 1.6 cm ($\frac{5}{8}$ in.) take a piece of gas piping of that size sharpened with a file at one end and, with the foam resting on a wood block, tap lightly with a hammer at the appropriate spot.

## Refurbishing deep-buttoned work with loose filling

When refurbishing a deep-buttoned upholstered piece, it will be found frequently that the base or groundwork is in sound condition, the upper filling and covering only needing attention. If this is the case, take off the top covering and buttons and cut the twine ties to enable you to remove the hair filling; this should reveal the groundwork marking. The top covering should be smoothed out, if possible ironed, so that it may be used as a template for marking the button positions on the new covering. Filling which has been removed should be 'teased' or opened to bring back its resilience and enable it to push out the pleating in definite lines without undue wrinkling.

### *Planning deep buttoning*

The basic principle of deep diamond buttoning is that the button positions need to be planned and marked first on the base or ground hessian and then, in relation to the marking on the groundwork, the reverse side of the outer cover. In doing the latter, an extra allowance must be given over the groundwork sizes to give 'fullness' for the pleating which is necessary to form the diamonds.

The length and width of the intended diamonds should be of a suitable size in relation to the overall size of the piece being worked. It is a common fault to make diamonds too large or too small. Diamonds may be square, i.e. equal length and width, or elongated, with the length greater than the width. In assessing the button positions and the appropriate size of the diamonds, it is good practice to experiment with loose tacks, which can be removed later, pushed into the base hessian before doing any marking, as this will avoid having a mass of marks or lines which could be confusing if marked wrongly.

Loose tacks can be placed in lines in a staggered formation so that it can be seen where complete or half diamonds will fit into the scheme of buttoning horizontally and vertically. Where buttons come at the ends of rows near the edges, the sizes of the diamonds should be adjusted so that the last button in the row is approximately half the width of a diamond

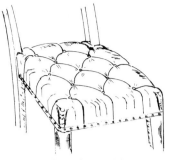

*Diagram 60* Buttoned chair
seat

from the edge (*diagram 60*). Having the end buttons too close or too far from the edges of seats or back will give an unbalanced appearance. This applies to the front and sides of seats and top and sides of backs – the space beyond the back row of seat and bottom row of back buttons should be a little wider.

### Marking covering for fullness

After preparing and marking button positions on to the groundwork, the top covering should be prepared whilst the marking is still visible, before the second stuffing of hair is applied so that reference be made to it if necessary. The covering should be cut to the approximate size, being a little generous for the sake of safety. When calculating the size needed, take into consideration the amount of fullness which is to be allowed, together with a suitable allowance for tacking off around the sides and front.

The fullness needed can be judged by taking a measurement between two marked points over a cupped hand, as shown in figure 51. The hand may be held in a rather flattish cup shape to give the measurement for fairly shallow buttoning, or the hand may be held in a deeply cupped shape which will represent much deeper buttoning if transferred on to the covering.

When marking the covering, use flat tailor's chalk on the *reverse* side of the covering material, working from the vertical centre, measuring the button positions and spaces between buttons towards each side of the material, so that there will be an equal amount of material for tacking at each side. The marking of horizontal positions of buttons should be started from the front on seats; on backs or bed headboards it should be started from the topmost positions – in both cases ensuring that ample material is allowed for tacking at the extreme front of the seat or top edges of backs or headboards. An example of marking for diamond buttoning is shown in figure 52. It is very important that the lines marked on the material closely follow the weave of the material. The example shows marking for a bed headboard covering.

As a general guide, an average amount of additional covering measurement to allow over the groundwork measurement to give a suitable depth of sink for diamond buttoning would be 5 mm to each 2.5 cm of groundwork ($\frac{3}{16}$ in. to each inch), straight across between the markings (i.e. $\frac{1}{5}$ or 20 per cent approximately). For example, should the groundwork measurements for the diamonds be $15.3 \times 16.5$ cm ($6 \times 6\frac{1}{2}$ in.), the measurement for the covering marking would be $18.3 \times 19.8$ cm ($7\frac{1}{8} \times 7\frac{11}{16}$ in.).

*Figure 51* Assessing the amount of fullness for buttoning over a cupped hand

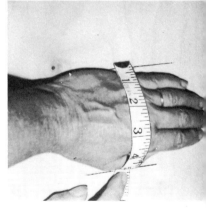

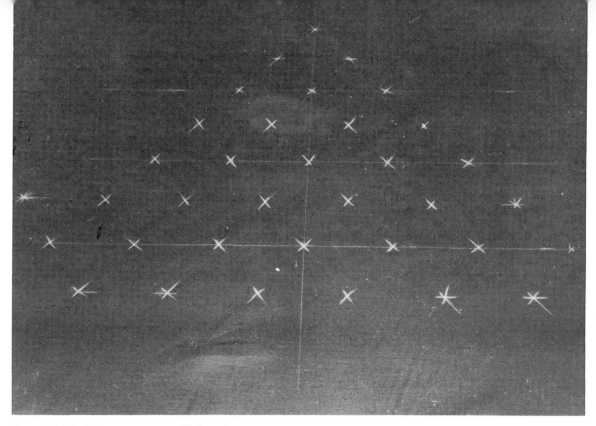

*Figure 52* Marking on covering for buttoned bed headboard

### Twine ties

With the covering prepared, before in-filling with the stuffing, if the base is first stuffed and stitched in scrim, holes should be made in the scrim at the marked button positions, and the holes should be sufficiently large to enable the buttons to sink into the hole when pulled down with the twine. Snip two or three threads of the scrim and force a finger into the cut threads and move it around to shift the filling and to enlarge the hole to make a bed deep enough for the button to sink lower than the surface of the scrim. Lengths of strong twine should be passed through the hole made at each button position using a long, straight, fine buttoning needle, taking needle and twine down through the base canvas and returning a small distance away, approximately 5 mm ($\frac{1}{4}$ in.), so that when pulled tightly the twine will not break away from the hessian.

A safety measure against the twine pulling away from the hessian is to slip a small cutting of webbing or hessian or other material into the loop of twine under the base hessian (*diagram 2*). This will be an insurance against the hessian threads breaking and allowing the button to become detached either whilst working upon it or at some later date whilst being used – a most annoying occurrence. Twine underneath the base hessian should be a running line and not knotted at this point because the button is held down by making a 'slip knot' (*diagram 62*), with the two ends of twine on the surface of the work. One end should be left long and the other shorter to give sufficient length to enable the knot to be slipped down and handled easily when easing the button down to the desired length.

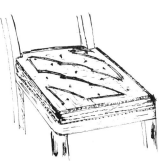

*Diagram 61* Bridle ties sewn
loosely into stuffing scrim

### Second stuffing

Bridle ties (*figure 36 on page 49 and diagram 61*) should now be sewn into
the scrim with loops approximately 15 to 20 cm (6 to 8 in.) long, running the
loops diagonally between lines of buttons instead of straight across as
normal with stuffed work.

Ample filling, well teased with plenty of life, should be in-filled over the
first stuffing ensuring that the twines inserted for the buttons are not
covered with filling but emerge through the surface of the loose stuffing
immediately above their positions in the scrim. Insufficient or poor quality
filling will not give the basis for good pleating as it will be found difficult to
attain clean, straight, single pleats between the buttons and a good deal of
wrinkling of the covering will be unavoidable.

Over the filling two or three layers of cellulose skin wadding, known
sometimes as sheet wadding, should be laid loosely with the twines pushed
through holes and poked through the wadding. It is essential that the
wadding be laid very loosely over the filling to enable it to pleat in the same
way as the covering.

### Buttoning the covering

Starting with the centre buttons and the centre diamonds, thread both the
twines at each button position through the covering at the appropriate
points – be especially careful to ensure that the first twines worked are
through the covering at the correct positions as it is very easy to make an
error at this juncture.

Pass *one* of the twines through the wire loop of the button, or, if a tufted
back button, pass a fine buttoning needle and *one* twine only through the
fabric tuft, and tie a slip knot with the two twines. Ease the knot partially
down only, leaving a small amount of tightening down to be done at a later
stage. Work out from the centre tying in all the buttons in their respective
positions and, whilst easing down the buttons, form the pleating diagonally
between each button. The flat end of an upholsterer's regulator is ideal for
the purpose of persuading the material to fold at the right places or even the
flat handle of a spoon or similar instrument will be suitable.

Pleating should be folded forward or towards the front of seating, and
folded downwards on backs or bed headboards.

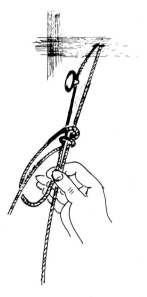

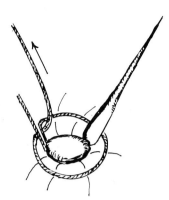

*Diagram 63* Finally tying off
twine around the sunken
button

*Diagram 62* Forming the 'slip'
knot

With all buttons in position and partially pulled down and the pleating formed, the covering at the sides and front or top should be temporary tacked into position. At the same time, adjust the pleats from the outside rows of buttons horizontally or vertically as opposed to diagonally as with the inner pleats forming the diamonds. The buttons may now be eased down finally to the maximum necessary and tied off (*diagram 63*), finishing with the final tacking of the covering on the underside or outside of the frame.

## Deep buttoning with foam interior

The average D.I.Y. home-upholstery enthusiast keen to attempt some form of deeply buttoned upholstery project generally will look upon working with foam as a more attractive and easier proposition than working with the traditional loose fillings – with the added advantages that foam is easier to obtain and, of course, cleaner to work with.

In a number of instances when refurbishing an item, foam may be used to replace the second stuffing, usually hair, of a normal stuffed seat or back, provided that the base springing and first stuffing and stitching is in sound order. In this situation the existing markings on the groundwork, which will be exposed on removal of the old top stuffing, should be copied on to the sheet foam which has already been cut to a suitable size. Ensure that the marking it centred on the piece of foam and that the foam has been cut fractionally oversize rather than the exact size, as foam will always tend to reduce in size when being tied down. Then, where the marking shows the button positions, holes should be punched into the foam as described on page 82, to enable the buttons to sink into the foam, rather than let the buttons pull the foam down and reduce its depth.

The thickness of foam necessary if being placed on an existing stuffed seat would be 3.8 cm ($1\frac{1}{2}$ in.) minimum. If working on to a flat, solid base, such as plywood or chipboard without any existing filling, the thickness of foam should be a minimum of 7.5 cm (3 in.). A firm density foam should be used for seating purposes, with a lighter density for the buttoning of backs.

## Buttoning with leather or simulated leather

Working with leather or simulated leather (coated fabrics) on any form of upholstery is, of course, more difficult than working with a soft, woven fabric. Errors or faults made when using the latter can often be corrected without leaving any tell-tale signs, but with leather or simulated leather, due to the nature of the material, it is difficult to do this. It is, therefore, more important to be exact and precise when taking measurements or cutting and machining and finally when applying the covering to the upholstery.

Leather produced these days is much softer and easier to work than that produced some years ago. The same applies to coated fabrics, such as P.V.C. (polyvinyl chloride) and polyurethane-coated fabrics. Whilst simulated leathers are reasonably easy to purchase from many sources and are sold by the metre (lineal measure), purchasing leather suitable for upholstery work in the quantity usually required is rather more difficult. Leather processors (curriers) generally are not keen to sell quantities less than a half skin cut down the backbone (lengthways down the centre of the skin). The average size of a full skin is approximately 4.47 to 4.65 sq. m (48 to 50 sq. ft), although larger or smaller skins are available.

One of the problems of using leather is estimating the quantity needed as, invariably, it is not possible to avoid a certain amount of wastage due to the unevenness of the outer edges of the skin and the improbability of being able to purchase the precise amount required. This does mean a much higher outlay for covering than would be the case with a coated simulated leather or soft woven fabric which generally can be cut and used with very little waste.

When using a very soft leather or thin simulated leather, such as polyurethane-coated fabric, for deep-buttoning work it is advisable to stick a small square of cotton or linen fabric 1.3 cm ($\frac{1}{2}$ in.) approximately as a reinforcing patch on the underside of the covering where the needle and twine will penetrate. This will prevent the buttons from pulling through the leather, etc., if a good deal of tension is given to the twine in sinking the button. Also with leather and coated fabrics creases should be carefully hammered into the covering diagonally between the button positions as this will assist the pleating to set and lie flat. The diagonal creases should be made to the outside line of buttons *only*, from these the creases should project straight out at right angles to the edges of the leather. When hammering in the creases using a large-faced hammer, care should be taken not to damage the leather.

# Working with leather

As mentioned earlier, present-day leathers, being very soft and supple, are ideal for the covering of upholstery, using foam filling for the main upholstery and the loose cushions. Unlike woven fabric, the visual appearance of an upholstered item covered in leather is often enhanced by the wrinkled or creased finish which is purposely contrived to give an appearance of exceptional comfort.

Although the tendency of modern upholstery designing is to demand straight-forward plain seaming, the welted seam (or piped seam) does stand up to harder and longer wear. Machine stitching of leather should be undertaken using a much longer stitch than that used for fabric and with a finer needle. Very close stitching with a coarse needle will make the seam weaker by the close perforations of the needle.

## Re-stretching leather

When refurbishing an upholstered chair, settee or even loose seats, it may be found that whilst the original leather may be still sound with years of further wear, it has become stretched and loose in areas where the body weight has been concentrated, i.e. in the centre of seats and backs and, in the case of covered arms, along the top of the scroll. Attempting to rectify this by re-stretching by hand, generally will prove difficult, as most of the older leather upholstery will have been covered with a much thicker and tougher skin than is used today.

Nor will re-shaping be completely effective by putting extra filling under the leather, so it is necessary to apply a gentle but firm stretching to the surrounding areas. This is best accomplished by using the upholsterer's hide strainer as mentioned on page 16. This is a specialist pincer-like tool with wide jaws which have serrations on their inner faces to grip the leather when closed firmly. If this tool is not available, a pair of 'Mole' grips will make a good substitute, although they do not have such wide jaws as the normal hide strainer. Figure 56 shows 'Mole' grips being used in this way for re-stretching the leather on a dining chair loose seat, but care must be taken not to overstretch the leather as it will split easily, particularly at corners.

When using either the hide strainers or the substituted 'Mole' grips, they should be used in the right hand to apply the tension to the leather. When the tension has been applied, the edge of the leather should be held firmly in place with the fingers and thumb of the left hand, as shown in figure 53, the straining tool is then exchanged for a hammer and a 1.3 cm ($\frac{1}{2}$ in.) tack is hammered in at the appropriate spot to hold firmly the stretched leather.

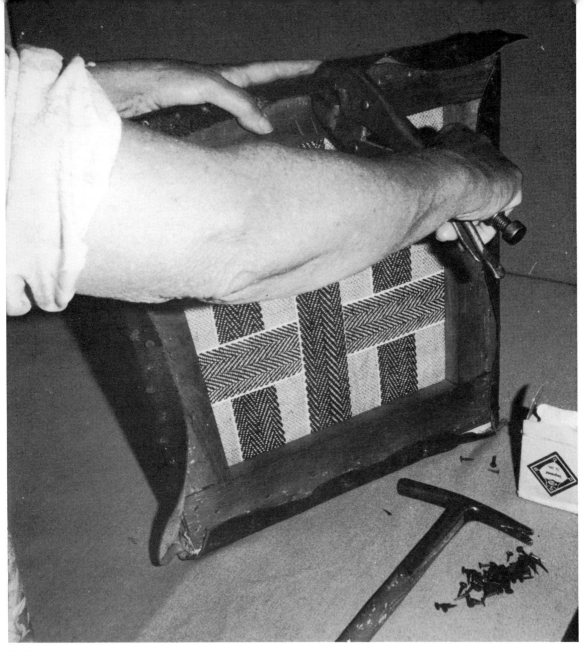

## Finishing and trimming leather upholstery

*Figure 53* Using 'Mole' grips to tension leather on loose seat

Unlike fabric, leather or P.V.C. is very difficult to slip-stitch at edges where the material has to be folded and finished (in such places as outside backs, outside arms, facings, etc.), so it is necessary to use the traditional brass or oxidized plain domed or fancy nails. The cheapest method of purchasing these if a large number is required is in boxes of 1000, as the professional upholsterer buys them, but most D.I.Y. stores will sell smaller packets, but these, of course, work out a good deal more expensive.

The normal plain domed oxidized or brass nail which is used has a 1 cm ($\frac{7}{16}$ in.) diameter head with a shank or pin of approximately 1.5 cm ($\frac{5}{8}$ in.).

Some difficulty will be found in hammering these nails in straight without bruising or denting the heads. It is, therefore, advisable to practise hammering a few nails into a spare piece of timber in a straight line in order to avoid damaging the leather with bent nails and to pick up the knack of hitting them in the centre where the pin is situated. Frequently these nails are applied as 'close' nailing, i.e. where the nails are put in adjacent and touching each other. With this method, the siting of the nails at the ends of the rows need to be calculated before they are reached. It is a good principle to hammer in the last two nails when approximately 5 to 6 cm away from the end (2 to $2\frac{1}{2}$ in.), then plan the positions for the intervening nails. In some instances it may be necessary to leave fractional spaces between the last few nails or perhaps a nail may need the head hammering slightly narrower to fit in as in figure 54 where the fifth nail from the left has been treated in this way.

*Figure 54* Positioning of close nailing

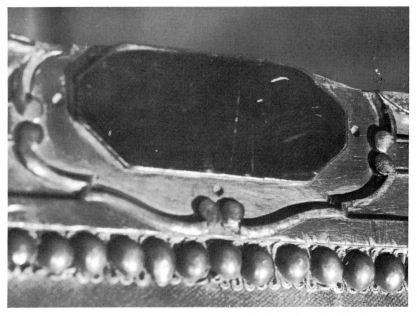

'Space' nailing, which is a more economical and probably the most popular method of nailing for the finishing of leather upholstery, uses optional spacing. To attain the professional look, however, the spacing should be regular and is best measured and marked on the leather with pencil or metal dividers.

Where leather is to be nailed as a finish, the method of tacking prior to the nailing is important. For close nailing, *gimp pins* (*diagram 1*) only should be hammered home so that the domed heads of the nails will cover their small heads. With space nailing gimp pins should also be used but left as temporary tacking so that as the nails are put in, the gimp pins that are positioned where a nail is to be sited can be hammered home, but those which are sited in the spaces can be removed. The removal of some gimp pins will leave minute holes but there will be practically no sign of these when the nailing is in position. P.V.C. banding, 1.2 cm ($\frac{1}{2}$ in.) wide is also available, which is a convenient way of covering tacks when space nailing into a rebate.

Alternatively, it is still possible to obtain covered studs with matching banding from upholstery material suppliers. Studs are made in the same way as covered upholstery buttons and are the same size as the normally used button but, instead of having a wire loop or tuft at the back of the button for tying, a 1.3 cm ($\frac{1}{2}$ in.) tack is incorporated in the button which is then referred to as a stud. These must be carefully hammered home without bruising the surface at the appropriate spacing with or without banding (*figure 60*).

*Figure 55* Removing old nailing with sharp screwdriver prior to re-upholstery

*Figure 56* Studs and banding
on panel back

## Leather cushions

In making leather or simulated leather cushions for upholstered items, because these materials are impermeable, or airtight, it is essential that provision be made for the escape of air from the cushion interior, *particularly* when using a foam filling but also even if using feathers or down, although then the problem is not quite so acute! Allowance for the escape of air can be made in three ways.

a  By inserting plastic or brass air vents in the side borders before the cushion is filled. The brass vents need a special tool to fit a ring on the inside of the border, but the plastic type can be easily fitted by hand (*diagrams 64a and b*).

a        b

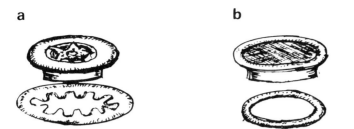

*Diagram 64* Air vents, to allow escape of air from leather or P.V.C. cushion, (a) plastic (b) brass

**b** By making up part of the underside covering of the cushion in a soft breathable fabric to match the leather or P.V.C., the front covering piece being approximately 12.5 to 15 cm (5 to 6 in.) wide with the remainder of the base as fabric machined across the front panel of leather.

**c** By making the back border only of a soft breathable fabric, reaching from the two corners across the back.

Any of these methods will help to prevent splitting of the seaming which can happen through air being suddenly forced out without any venting being provided.

## Protection of leather

After having worked hard on refurbishing an upholstered piece covered in leather, it makes good sense to protect the leather against deterioration and the drying out of its natural oil. Figure 57 shows an attractive writing chair which was completely covered in leather but, as the result of neglect, and through being situated in a constantly warm and dry centrally-heated office, the leather has completely perished and has torn away in large pieces.

*Figure 57* Result of neglect – perishing of the leather covering

93

To preserve leather it should be given an occasional treatment of leather skin food which will replace the natural oil and will enable the leather to retain its suppleness over a period of many years. An excellent preparation to be recommended for this protection is marketed by Messrs Connolly Bros, the leather processors of London. The preparation is supplied in small jars and should be obtainable at any good furnishing store dealing in leather upholstery.

# Show-wood upholstery

The term 'show-wood upholstery' refers generally to an upholstered item which has an amount of polished surface visible with the upholstery covering freque ;tly tacked adjacent to the polished surface with a line of gimp or braid to hide the tacks. The show-wood piece may be a small chair, fireside chair, easy chair, or settee. Figure 58 shows a leather show-wood easy chair.

Show-wood work needs far more careful handling than the usual stuffover type of upholstery, as there are a number of pitfalls which can cause damage to the delicate nature of the show-wood frame in some way. This type of upholstered frame tends to be more lightly constructed than their stuffover counterparts. Tensioning of the various materials needs to be undertaken with care. When tensioning the webbing, the 'bat'-type webbing stretcher often will need to bear on the polished surface to apply sufficient tension and, therefore, a pad of wadding or felt should be placed between the webbing stretcher and the polished surface to prevent marking the show-wood frame. Do *not* use a pad of hessian or any form of woven material as the weave will cause an imprint of the yarn on the polish due to the pressure applied. Also, do not strain the webbing as tightly as one would when webbing a stuffover frame.

When tacking along a polished, rebated edge, use small tacks, i.e. 1 cm ($\frac{3}{8}$ in.) fine so that strenuous hammering is not necessary to knock the tack home. Also, to avoid hitting the polished, rebated edge, develop the knack of guiding the face of the hammer with the thumbnail so that the hammer slides along the nail on to the head of the tack and not on to the polish. With a little practice the edge of the rebate can be felt with the inner tip of the thumb whilst holding the fabric to be tacked at the spot where the tack is to be hammered in. A cabriole hammer, which is a hammer with a smaller than normal face, is a great help in tacking into polished rebates (*diagram 38 on page 60*).

*Figure 58* A show-wood
leather-covered easy chair

## Refurbishing a pin-stuffed seat

Probably one of the most delicate upholstery tasks in the show-wood field one can undertake is the pin-stuffed or pin-cushion seat. This type of upholstered seat is formed in a variety of styles of light chairs, i.e. bedroom chairs and occasional chairs, etc. (*diagram 65*). A style of chair which is particularly attractive, but needs a great deal of care to work upon and refurbish, is what is popularly known as a 'corner chair'. The origin of this style dates back to about 1720, when it was known as a writing chair and frequently had a rounded front to the seat so that the legs fit either side.

Pin-stuffed upholstery is worked on the top side of the seat members which have shallow rebates on which to fit the webbing, hessian, calico undercover, top covering and gimp. The limited width of the rebate, usually seldom more than 1 cm ($\frac{3}{8}$ in.), added to its shallowness, 2 to 3 mm ($\frac{1}{8}$ to $\frac{1}{4}$ in.), makes it very difficult to tack all the materials without splitting the timber of the edge of the rebate or overlapping the polished edge. It is advisable in this instance to use small tacks, i.e. 1 cm ($\frac{3}{8}$ in.) fine throughout to tack *all* the materials: the webbing (not folded in this instance), hessian, calico undercover (not folded), and top covering (not folded). If a stapling gun is available it will be found to be advantageous over the tacking method with less danger of splitting the timber.

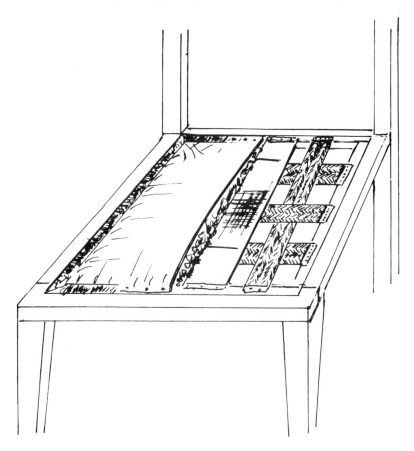

*Diagram 65* 'Pin' stuffed or 'pin cushion' seat upholstery

Stripping of the old gimp and covering must be undertaken with great care and it is very important to strip tacks out in the direction of the grain of the timber (along the length of the member). Failure to take this precaution *will* result in pieces of the rebate splitting away and will make the re-upholstery work more difficult. Take special care at the corners of the rebate not to let the ripping tool slip over the polished edge beyond the rebate because, if it does, a nasty score will appear across the polish which will be difficult to eradicate and will leave an unsightly blemish.

Start the re-upholstery by tacking a piece of black linen over the open area, tacking along the four sides to present a neat and tidy appearance to the underside. This also prolongs the life of the webbing and hessian. The black linen should be folded over using 1 cm ($\frac{3}{8}$ in.) fine tacks.

Use a good quality black and white linen webbing, rather than the inferior brown jute webbing, and $3 \times 3$ strands interlaced are required. With a very shallow rebate, tack the webbing in this instance single thickness only, with *no* fold over. Since there is no fold over, you should make sure that the small tacks, 1 cm ($\frac{3}{8}$ in.) fine, are well and truly home flat so that they hold the web strands firmly.

A very light tension only should be applied to the webbing. In fact, with a strong hand one can easily give sufficient tension without using the webbing stretcher, hammering the tacks in at an angle to tension the webbing as the tacks enter further into the timber (*diagram 66*).

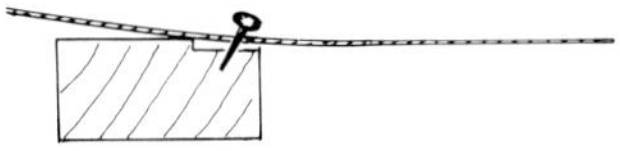

*Diagram 66* Slight tensioning by inserting tacks at an angle

A good quality hessian should be laid and tacked over the webbing, again using 1 cm ($\frac{3}{8}$ in.) fine tacks. This should be folded over but kept away from the polished edge of the rebate without tacking too close to the inside edge. It is advisable to keep observing the underside of the members to see if any splitting is occurring and, if so, the offending tacks should be removed and replaced in a different position.

Horse hair is the traditional filling for this particular type of seat, but this can be replaced successfully by foam if desired, using 2.5 cm (1 in.) thickness with an underlay of 1.3 cm ($\frac{1}{2}$ in.), in the centre area to give slight doming. An undercover of calico or lining should be tacked over the filling, first temporary tacking centres and then following with a firm tension into each corner diagonally to remove fullness and accentuate the doming.

If horse hair or other loose filling has been used, wadding will be needed over the undercovering. It is always better to apply wadding *over* the undercovering rather than under it because, if placed over the loose filling, it will tend to wrinkle or fold with the contraction of the filling. Placed over the undercover, it will remain smooth without any movement of the filling taking place. The wadding should be trimmed away well clear of the edge of the rebate so that it will not protrude beyond the edge of the final covering; it is difficult to trim away with a knife or scissors once the covering is in place.

If using a foam filling, however, wadding is not necessary and, if desired, the undercover may be omitted, although the seat will be better for the extra work involved. The underside edges of the foam should be given a slight chamfer with a little cut away to avoid the edge being too bulky.

Again, the covering should be well temporary tacked, using a line between the front and back corners of the seat as the centre of the fabric. But when temporary tacking start at the centre of each side, working to the corners again to clean the fullness and tighten the covering. When finally tacking home, ensure the tacks are positioned so that the gimp will cover them. It is advisable to have a short cutting of the gimp to be used so that the tacking can be tested whilst working along each side.

Using an adhesive, such as 'Copydex', or some other non-contact type, carefully work from the back corner applying the adhesive to short stretches approximately 10 to 15 cm (4 to 5 in.) at a time, smoothing the gimp into its position with the fore-finger or thumb, then holding it in position with a temporary tack or two (preferably gimp pins) which can be left for a few hours whilst the adhesive hardens and then removed.

The fold of the gimp at the corners should be neatly mitred with a gimp pin placed under the fold so that it is hidden. The final gimp pins at the last fold-over should be inserted so that they are covered by the loose yarn of the gimp. This is usually easy to open up to allow the gimp pins (usually two are needed) to be tapped in position whilst the yarn is held open with the pointed end of an upholsterer's skewer or needle, and this will avoid an unsightly finishing join in the gimp.

Before attempting to use adhesive, lay a protective sheet over the covering to catch any stray drops of adhesive. It is better to be safe than sorry after the event – invariably they will drop in the centre of the seat.

# Fluting

The replacement or recovering of a 'fluted' or 'plumed' back for a chair or settee may be undertaken in various ways. Generally the original fluted covering will have been made up as a separate unit and laid upon either a sprung base groundwork, or upon a firm base made up with webbing only. In most cases the supporting groundwork will be in sound condition requiring no attention, this being best left undisturbed if possible.

The origin and the advantage of a fluted back is similar to that of the deep-buttoned back, in that it allows fullness in the covering of a curved or 'spoon' shaped back to be dissipated or removed in a decorative fashion but, as in the case of deep buttoning, it is nowadays often only used for decorative reasons.

A secret in achieving successful fluting work is that the dividing lines of stitching between the flutes should be tensioned as tightly as possible in the vertical direction (i.e. from the bottom of the lines at the base of the back to the top), with the object of keeping the lines straight and removing any wrinkling of the covering. Figure 59 shows an occasional chair back which has a fluted finish on a firm base of webbing. As this particular covering has a dark background with a bright decorative pattern, the lines between the raised flutes are machined through the top of the covering, with a good matching thread, on to the hessian used to back the fluting prior to filling. Widths of the flutes are narrower at the base than at the top to conform with the tapering of the back towards the base. With this method of working, the machine lines should be drawn finely on the surface of the covering with chalk at the appropriate widths to enable the machinist to follow the lines accurately.

The depth of the sunken machine lines between the flutes when in position on the back will be governed by the difference between the widths of the flutes drawn on the hessian and the covering, i.e. the fullness allowed on the covering to give doming to the flute. This fullness, or extra width, of covering should be between 1.3 and 1.8 cm ($\frac{1}{2}$ and $\frac{3}{4}$ in.).

## Fluting tool

An aluminium fluting sleeve was used to fill the flutes shown in figure 59. This tool, frequently used by professional upholsterers, consists of a long tube in two halves along its length of approximately 75 cm (2 ft 6 in.) which is hinged at the base. In use, the tube is opened (as the jaws of a crocodile), the filling laid along one half of the tube, the jaws are closed tightly compressing the filling, and the whole is then slipped into the channels of the prepared fluted back cover, filling one channel at a time.

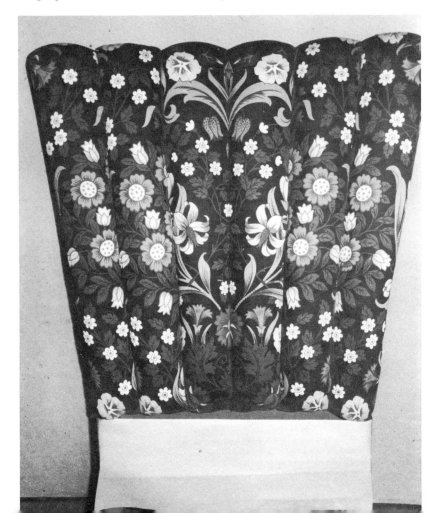

*Figure 59* Fluted chair back

99

*Figure 60* A simple fluting
tool

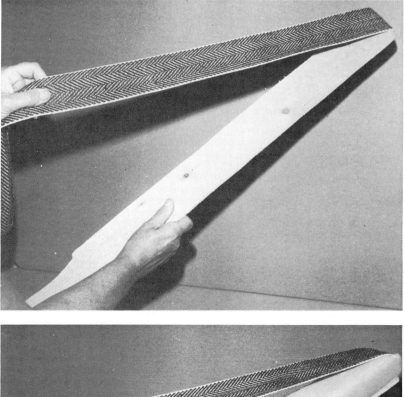

*Figure 61* Filling in place on
fluting tool

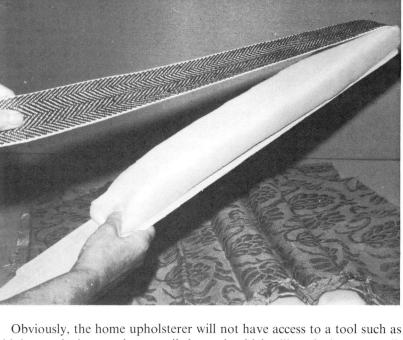

Obviously, the home upholsterer will not have access to a tool such as this but a substitute tool may easily be made which will work almost as well. Figure 60 shows a simple home-made filler consisting of a length of wood with webbing attached at one end. The filling is laid evenly along the flat surface of the wood, preferably in a continuous length. The webbing is pulled over the top of the filling and the free end of the webbing is held tightly with the right hand, which is also holding the shaped handle of the filler (*figure 61*). The filling is then inserted and gently pushed along the open tube of fluting until it reaches the top of the covering, while being held firmly at the entry point (*figure 62*) the webbing is then carefully withdrawn through the top of the channel so as not to disturb the filling, after which the wood is withdrawn, and the process is begun again for the next flute. It is not necessary to fill the two outside flutes in this manner, as these should not be machined as channels but left open and filled when the covering is in position on the back and then tacked along the outside of the frame.

Foam may be used successfully for this operation; it should, of course, be of sufficient thickness, or rolled, to give the depth of flute as required.

*Figure 62* Inserting fluting tool with filling into channel of covering

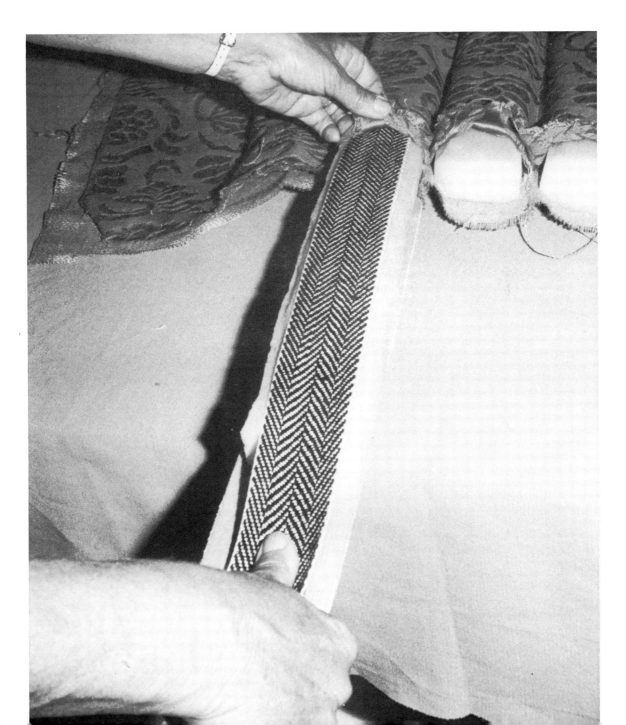

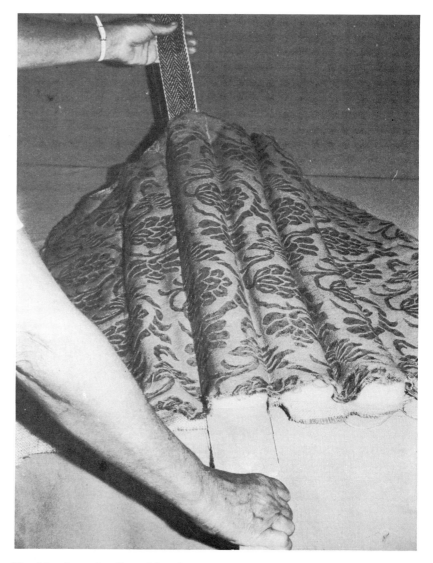

*Figure 63* Withdrawing of fluting tool

## Positioning the fluted back

When placing the prepared fluted back on to the frame it is necessary to measure and mark centres, and temporary tack accurately so that the two outer lines are equal distance from the side rails. Just sufficient tension should be given laterally, tensioning the backing hessian just enough to bring the flutes to their intended width; they will have reduced a little with the pressure of the filling within. The hessian should now be tacked.

Vertical, machined lines only should be tensioned as tightly as possible, stretching the hessian and the covering together, tacking at top and bottom of the lines allowing the covering between to form its own domed shape and working any looseness sideways into the machined line. Filling for the two outside flutes should now be laid into position and the loose covering pulled over and tacked.

## Alternative methods of preparing fluted coverings

Diagram 67 shows an alternative method of preparing covering for fluting, the covering being machined on the reverse side on a fold instead of singly through the face side of the covering, so that the machining line is not visible as perhaps it may be in the previous method. An allowance of approximately 0.8 to 1 cm ($\frac{5}{16}$ to $\frac{3}{8}$ in.) for the fold must be made when chalking the lines on the covering. Filling may be inserted into the fluted channels with the home-made tool as described in the previous method.

A further method of preparing such a back, is by laying the filling in position on the hessian after marking, and then machining the covering down the fold whilst compressing the filling. It is rather more difficult to achieve straight lines using this method.

*Diagram 67* Machining covering for fluting to hide machined line

*Diagram 68* Fluted seat cover on deep foam interior

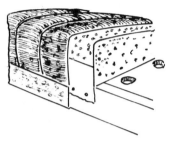

# Refurbishing a wing easy chair

An example of a purchase at reasonable cost at a second-hand furniture sale room is shown in figure 64. A square-framed, pad-arm, wing easy chair, obviously needing major re-upholstery work and recovering. This purchase is an ideal example of a project which, with slight modification to the frame, is well within the scope of the handyman/woman and can be re-upholstered using a more simplified method of upholstery than the original, utilising foam and Pirelli resilient rubber webbing to appear as in diagrams 69 and 70.

## Testing the frame

Before purchase, the chair was tested for undue movement or slackness in the joints of the frame. This is best done by placing a knee on the front edge of the seat to hold the chair steady and applying pressure on the front edges of the wings, arms and on the top of the back. This example was found to be in sound condition.

*Figure 64* Second-hand chair
for re-upholstery

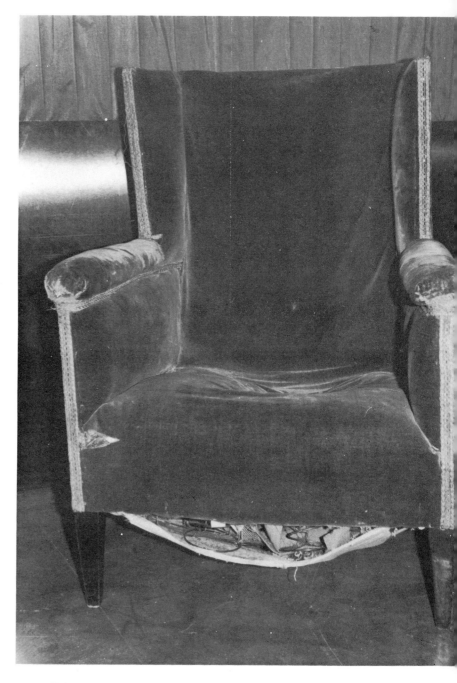

It will be noted that the original seat of the chair was upholstered as a
'full' seat, that is, constructed for use without a full-size seat cushion in the
seat. For the purpose of this project and the appearance of the chair, the
upholstery will be altered to include a cushion in the seat which will enable a
more simplified method of upholstery to be used, allowing the use of Pirelli
resilient rubber webbing and foam.

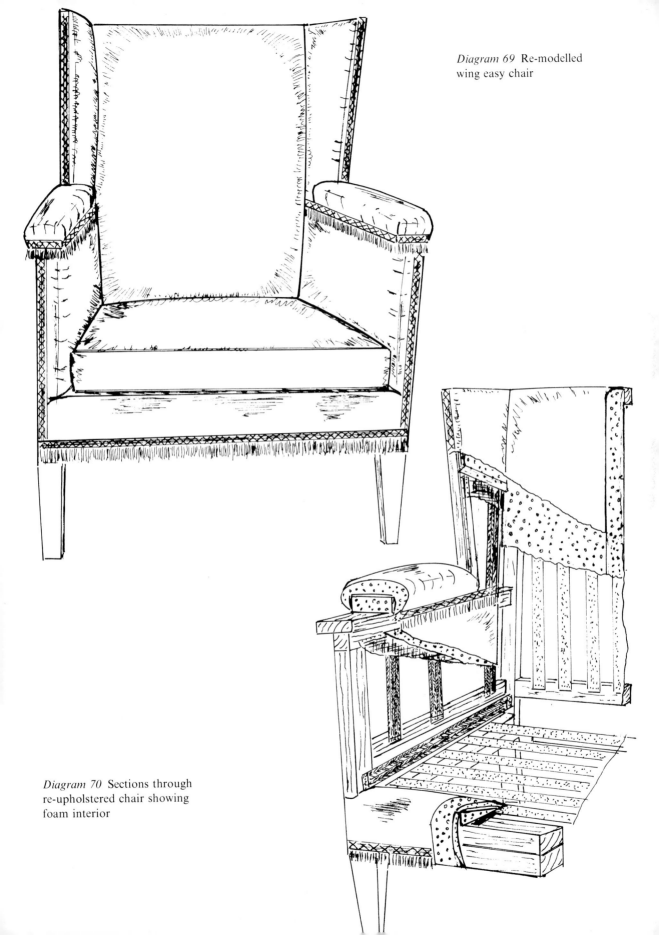

*Diagram 69* Re-modelled
wing easy chair

*Diagram 70* Sections through
re-upholstered chair showing
foam interior

## Stripping and frame modification

The first step in the work is to strip off carefully all the old original upholstery down to the bare frame (*figure 65*). As an insurance against future deterioration of the joints, which is always possible with an old frame, flat steel reinforcing plates were screwed to the outside of the frame at the joints of the front arms and base rail and the base of the front rail of the wing and top arm members. These can be seen screwed in position as shown in figure 65. They are further illustrated in diagrams 12, 13 and 14 (*see page 24*). At this stage the modification should be made to the frame.

a  Lengths of wood should be firmly screwed along the top of each of the arm rails (*diagram 70*). These should be the same length as the arm from the base of the wing to the front of the arm rail by 6.5 cm ($2\frac{1}{2}$ in.) wide by 1.5 cm ($\frac{5}{8}$ in.) thickness.

b  Lengths of timber should be firmly screwed along the top of the front and both side base rails. These should be the same length and width as these rails by 4 cm ($1\frac{1}{2}$ in.) deep, and the heads of the screws may be sunken in these rails to avoid using over-length screws. These additional members will give added height to allow rubber webbing to be used, obviating the need for deep coil springing as used in the original.

*Figure 65* Chair stripped to basic framework

106

Whilst the timber for the arms could be of a soft wood, it is vitally important that the additional timber secured to the base seat rails is hard wood and is screwed in position very firmly.

Six strands of 5 cm (2 in.) Pirelli resilient rubber webbing should be tensioned *across* the seat over the new rails screwed to the base rails at a tension of 8 to 10 per cent. The webbing should be tacked to the outside faces so that the tacking points and cut ends of the webbing will not be visible on the inside of the chair. The strands of webbing should be spaced equally.

## Pad and panel

With the preparation of the frame completed and the seat webbing in place, upholstery may now be begun, commencing with the arm pads and inside panels. Diagram 70 shows a cut-through section of the upholstery of the pad and panel with the extra timber added. Three lengths of linen/jute webbing should be tacked/stapled to the arm stay rail using 1 cm ($\frac{3}{8}$ in.) tacks, being hand-tensioned only, and tacked to the face of the upper arm, the back length of web being tacked approximately 1.8 cm ($\frac{3}{4}$ in.) from the back leg and running parallel with it. Hessian, to cover the inside panel area, should be tacked from the arm stay rail and tensioned by hand and tacked to the face of the upper arm and front rails. The rear of the hessian should be folded under and laid over the back web so that the fold is in line with the back edge of the web, the tacks at the top and bottom holding the fold tightly in place.

The position of the arm stay rail, which is the bottom of the arm, is too high for our modified method of upholstery so, in order to attain a lower line, a length of woven webbing should be tightly tensioned, being tacked on the inside face of the front arm member and inside back leg. The bottom line of this web should be approximately 2.5 cm (1 in.) above the rubber webbing line.

Cut a piece of 2.5 cm (1 in.) firm density foam to the same width and length as the additional piece of timber to form the arm pad, and stick it down to prevent movement. Overlay this with a piece of foam 1.3 cm ($\frac{1}{2}$ in.) thick, sufficiently large for it to lie over the side of the top piece and extend to the bottom and front edge of the pad, cutting out a small right-angled section at the corners to allow the edges to butt together so avoiding a bulky corner. One or two tacks may be put in along the bottom edge to hold the foam whilst the covering is being tacked. The covering should be taken under the base of the pad and tacked on the face of the original top arm rail, the front corners being pleated with one or two pleats, depending upon the type of covering.

Before laying in the panel foam, the covering should be 'back-tacked' with card or webbing tightly against the under-side of the pad along its whole length from front to back. 2.5 cm (1 in.) foam should be used to pad the panel, laying it over the lining hessian and allowing sufficient to tuck through the gap at the rear, adjacent to the back leg, and allowing it to flatten out on the face edge at the front. The foam and covering should be taken through the webbing at the bottom, tacking the covering on the outside of the base member leaving the front 15 cm (6 in.) untacked for the time being.

## Seat

As it is a cushion seat the front section of the seat only need be padded and covered if desired, allowing the seat cushion to rest on the rubber webbing beyond the covered area as is frequently done professionally. Diagrams 71a and b show the foam padding and the method of fixing the covering. The size of covering to be cut for the lip and front of seat should be the complete width of the chair by the amount needed to reach from the back of the first strand of webbing across, over the foam on the lip and front, to under the base of the front member.

Foam used should be a good firm density, preferably with an additional thickness immediately over the front rail to give deeper padding at that point. Covering should be tensioned tightly across and tacked on the outside of both side members. The bottom front part of the panel may now be finished off.

*Diagram 71* Fixing covering on front of cushion seat base

**a**

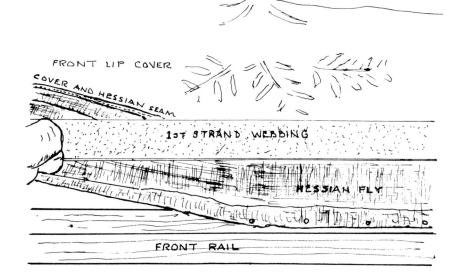

**b**

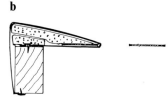

108

## Inside wing

The next stage is the inside wing, which should have a length of web tensioned from the arm rail, following the line of the web at the back of the inside panel to the inside of the top wing member and, like the panel, should be lined with hessian.

To soften the outside edge of the wing, tack a length of rubber draught excluder to the inside edge as shown in diagram 24 on page 37. This type of draught excluder is readily available in most hardwear stores.

Back-tack the covering for the inside wing along its bottom line, this being lined up with the base of the pad. Padding for the wing should be 2.5 cm (1 in.) thickness foam, and should be tucked through the gap at the back, as with the panel.

If it is intended to trim the wing edge with braid, as in figure 64, the covering should be tacked on the face edges. If the braid is to be omitted the covering should be tacked on the outside edge of the wing.

## Back

Foam for the inside back should be supported with seven strands of resilient rubber webbing 3.6 cm ($1\frac{1}{2}$ in.) wide, applied lengthwise from bottom to top of the back and tacked to the face of the back stay rail and face of the top member. Before fixing the rubber webbing to the bottom stay rail, check that the inside of the back when upholstered will not look too upright. If this looks as though it will, the base line of the back may easily be brought forward by the addition of a length of wood screwed securely to the face of the stay rail to which the rubber webbing can then be tacked. This will give an increased angle to the line of the inside back.

Using 7.5 cm (3 in.) soft density foam cut a piece to fit snugly between the arms and wings and from the seat webbing to the top back member, chamfering the top front edge of the foam to give a more rounded finish (*diagram 70*). To hold the foam in position tack flanges, or strips of lining or calico, approximately 10 cm (4 in.) wide to the back stay rail and top member, after sticking them to the top and bottom edges of the foam.

To enable the back covering to utilise half width of the cloth only, so economising with covering, extension or fly pieces of hessian or lining may be machined to both long sides of the back covering, and tucked through the gaps at the back of panels and wings. The covering at the base of the back should be taken through and tacked on the top of the back base member. The top of the back covering should be tacked to the outside of the top member, or top face if being finished with a braid on the edge.

Diagrams 52 and 53 (*see page 77 and 78*) show methods of cutting around the 'stiles' (rails obstructing the covering). Back covering should be tensioned lightly, just enough to take out the looseness.

## Outside covering

Before applying covering to the outside of the chair, hessian should be tacked in position over the open areas (i.e. outside arms, outside wings and outside backs) to reinforce the outer covering and prevent slackness if pressure is inadvertently applied to the covering. Sheet wadding should be laid evenly between the hessian and the covering. The outside coverings should be tacked on the edges of the frame if trimmed with a wide braid, otherwise it should be pinned to the extreme edges and slip-stitched leaving a plain seam.

If you do not desire a bottom covering of hessian or linen on the underside of the chair, the outside coverings should be folded *under* as they are being tacked around the under edge of the chair.

## Cushion

Foam for the seat cushion should be a good quality H.R. (high-resistant) seating density polyether, or seating quality latex foam, preferably 10 cm (4 in.) thickness or, to economise, a thinner 7.5 cm (3 in.) thickness may be utilised.

Foam cut from 7.5 cm (3 in.) or 10 cm (4 in.) sheet will provide a completely flat cushion which is more suitable for a modern style chair, whereas a domed cushion is more suitable for this traditional style, wing, easy chair. Doming of the cushion can be achieved by making the cushion from two 5 cm (2 in.) or 3.75 cm (1½ in.) thickness pieces of foam, with an additional inner thickness of 2.5 cm (1 in.) with chamfered edges sandwiched between the two thicker pieces (*diagram 72*). The two outer pieces should be stuck together around the perimeter edges with a good adhesive, and, in addition, having a band of linen or lining stuck around the face sides over the join on all four sides.

*Diagram 72* Making of domed seat cushion with foam

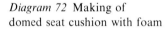

### Cutting the foam

Before cutting the foam a template should be cut from stout paper or card to the exact size of seat area into which the cushion is to fit, ensuring that if the width of the back is narrower than the width across the front edge, the taper is equal on both sides. The back line of the template should follow the shape of the bottom line of the back.

Hold the template firmly in place on the surface of the foam and mark around the edges using a felt tipped pen, remembering that this line is the finished size of the cushion. If the cushion is to be domed and made in two sections, both pieces should be marked accordingly.

Before cutting the foam, an additional line could be drawn to indicate the actual cutting line. This should allow for the small over-cutting amount as mentioned in an earlier chapter to enable the covering to keep its tension. Also, if doming is being given to the cushion surface, a slight additional amount should be allowed for the doming as this effect does tend to draw the edges in slightly. A slightly convex line should be drawn similar to that shown for cutting the covering (*diagram 73*). The foam may be cut with a broad bladed knife (*figure 14*).

### Cutting cushion covering

The template used for cutting the foam may also be used for marking the outer covering, not forgetting an allowance for seaming of 1 cm ($\frac{3}{8}$ in.) on each edge, and also a small amount in addition for doming if desired (*diagram 72*). Cushion seams may be piped, with the material for piping cut on the bias (*diagram 44a on page 66*). If ruching is to be used for trimming the cushion instead of piping, the seaming allowance when cutting the cushion covering should be omitted so that the cushion size will be a little smaller to allow the ruche to show to advantage and not be hidden between the arms and sides of the cushion.

The foam interior should be partly folded and inserted into the cushion case through one of the rear joins of the border and cushion panel. This should be subsequently slip-stitched.

## Feather/down cushion

If a feather/down cushion interior is preferred to a foam interior, rather more work will be involved, as an interior case made from waxed, down-proof cambric will need to be made to contain the feathers.

Make a template as for the foam interior. Use this to cut the interior case of cambric using the shiny waxed side for the inside of the case. Allow 2.5 cm (1 in.) on all sides of the template for a slight oversize allowance and seaming of the case. (This seaming should be turned in and edge stitched.) Also allow for the doming which occurs naturally with a well-filled feather and down cushion. Side borders of the case should also be cut over-size by 2 cm ($\frac{3}{4}$ in.). Sew the two division walls across the inside of the top and bottom panels connecting them before sewing the borders into position. This will form three chambers which will each hold their share of feathers/down permanently. The width of the division walls should be 3.6 cm ($1\frac{1}{2}$ in.) wider than the borders, being run down to the border width at their ends.

Openings for inserting the feathers should be left at one end of each of the chambers and when filled these should be sewn up by hand or machined. The completed filled interior should be oversize and larger than the template so that it will well fill the outer case (*diagram 74*).

FRONT

*Diagram 73* Extra allowance of covering for surface doming of cushion. Dotted line is allowance for seaming – outer solid line is additional allowance for doming

*Diagram 74* Filled waxed cambric interior case for chair seat

# Re-upholstery of a modern wing easy chair

Re-upholstery of the modern style wing chair, shown in figure 46 (*see page 69*) stripped down to its frame and basic springing should be a fairly straightforward undertaking. Modern materials can be used, i.e. foam and rubber webbing with a small quantity of linen or jute webbing and hessian, all of which can be purchased easily at relatively low cost. The quantity of covering fabric for such a chair and the cutting plan is shown in diagram 75.

*Diagram 75* Cover cutting plan for modern wing easy chair

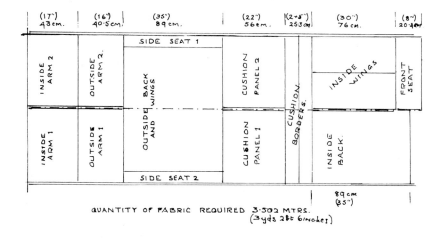

QUANTITY OF FABRIC REQUIRED 3·502 MTRS.
(3 yds 2ft 6 inches)

## Seat

In this particular example, the tension springing which supports the seat cushion should be replaced with 5 cm (2 in.) wide resilient rubber webbing, the springs first being unhooked and the long metal plates unscrewed, leaving the bare wood.

Six strands of rubber webbing should be applied *across* the seat at a tension of between $7\frac{1}{2}$ and 10 per cent, using 1.3 cm ($\frac{1}{2}$ in.) fine tacks. The webbing should be fixed, if possible, on the upper surface of the side rails. The chair frame shown has no arm stay rails at the base of the arms so it is easier to tension and fix the webbing in position. Some chairs may have an arm stay rail 2.5 or 5 cm (1 or 2 in.) above and parallel with the seat rail, making it difficult to tack the webbing to the upper surface and in such cases an alternative is to tack the webbing on the outer faces of the side members.

112

Diagrams 48 and 71 (*see pages 74 and 108*) show the method of covering the tacked ends of the webbing and covering the 'lip' or front of the seat, this being similar to the method used on the traditional style wing chair. Padding of the front edge should be with a piece of 2.5 cm (1 in.) thickness foam with a double thickness along the top surface of the timber (*diagram 71b*).

## Arms

The open area of the inside arm should now be webbed with two strands of woven webbing and lined with hessian, both of these being tacked along the inside edge of the top rail and left untacked temporarily along the base until the foam and the covering is in position; the hessian may be tacked on the front and back arm rails, leaving bottom back corner open.

To give added softness to the top of the arm, strips of foam equal to the width of the top arm members should be cut and stuck in position (*diagram 70 on page 105*) before the main larger piece to cover the whole inside arm is laid in position. Covering should be tacked on the outside of the arm members, leaving bottom back corner open.

## Back

As mentioned on p. 75, the back spring unit in figure 46 is in serviceable condition and does not need replacing. Cut a piece of foam 5 cm (2 in.) thickness (medium density) and lay it over the surface of the unit from the base wire to carry over the top wire. Stick a strip of calico or linen along the top and side edges of the foam and tack these to the frame and the sides of the back members respectively.

With the back foam in position, the size of the covering for the back should be calculated allowing enough for the side wings to be machined along the side lengths of the back, preferably with bias piping sewn in the join between the two. The back covering should reach from the bottom back rail to over the top and outside of the top back rail. The back covering should be wide enough to allow the piping between the back and wing to form a straight line from the base of the wing to the position where it traverses over the top rail. When fixing the back in position, the piped lines should be tensioned tightly along their length, passing the piping through the open areas at the bases of the wings.

## Wings

With the back and wings accurately in position, fold the wings back over the back covering. Fill in the open area of the wings with webbing and hessian, pad with 2.5 cm (1 in.) foam and tack covering off on the outside of the wing members after smoothing the covering.

## Outside covering

The outside arm covering should be back-tacked along the top outside edges and slip-stitched along the front edge. Outside back and wings covering should be cut in one piece. You may experience some difficulty in back-tacking the top line of the outside back and wings due to the curved shape and length of line. Hold this in position by pinning around the edges and slip-stitching with strong carpet thread. A bottoming of linen or hessian covering can be omitted if the outside covering is folded under whilst being tacked on the underside of the base members.

# Re-upholstery of a Chippendale period easy chair

The front jacket shows two Chippendale period reproduction chairs, one covered in tapestry and the other in leather, decorated with brass nailing – the traditional finish for that period style.

Figure 66 shows the basic beech show-wood frame with mahogany polished finish, needed to produce these chairs. This particular style was normally upholstered as a 'full' seat, so that a seat cushion is not necessary. The traditional method of upholstery of the seat is 'top' stuffing, i.e. upholstered on the top surface of the seat members. Frequently modern reproductions are produced with some form of springing in the seat, either with hand springing or the modern serpentine or sinuous spring (No-Sag or Zig-Zag), these being used in the back also.

Diagrams 76a, b, and c show sections through the chair upholstered in different ways. Diagram 76a, shows the chair upholstered using foam with resilient rubber webbing suspension for seat and back, with a loose seat cushion resting upon the seat webbing and a separate front lip and border as shown in diagram 71. Diagram 76b illustrates the chair upholstered completely in a traditional way, using coil springs in the seat, supported on woven webbing with fibre and hair filling, and stitched front edge as in diagrams 34 and 35 (*see page 58*). Diagram 76c shows the chair upholstered true to its original period style, full seated with the seat upholstery 'top' stuffed. This would have been completely upholstered with a good quality horse-hair filling throughout.

Diagram 77 shows a section through an arm pad showing scrim or stuffing canvas tacked along the centre of the arm member with a strip of webbing, with rolls formed along each side to give a slight overhang and a rounded edge.

114

*Figure 66* Chippendale chair frame

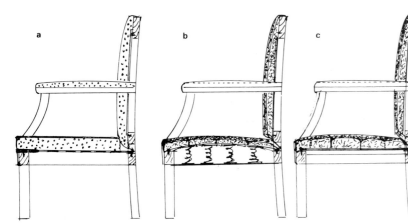

a  b  c

*Diagram 76* Chippendale period style chair: (a) upholstered with foam with loose seat cushion, (b) upholstered in traditional manner with sprung seat, (c) with full 'top' stuffed seat

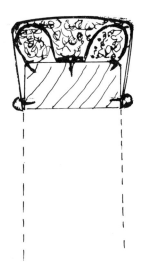

*Diagram 77* Section through arm pad upholstery

# Re-upholstery of a Victorian-style buttoned-back chair

Figures 67, 68, 69 and 70 show stages in the upholstery of a small, Victorian, deep buttoned-back chair.

Figure 67 shows the beechwood frame before upholstery. Practically every piece of timber used in the construction of the frame is shaped, so making it an expensive type of chair frame to produce. The front legs are turned and may be made from mahogany, walnut, etc., but frequently this type of leg is turned from beech, and subsequently stained in order to attain the desired colour to simulate a more expensive timber.

It will be noted that a number of the curved members have a very short grain length at radius sections and this makes the member very vulnerable to fracturing if hammered too severely or if too large a tack is being used. Great care should be taken to use the smaller tacks, i.e. 1 cm ($\frac{3}{8}$ in.) at the danger points, and a light hammering action. In addition, and as an extra safety precaution, the rail should be supported by holding with the hand to minimise vibration whilst hammering the tacks.

Figure 68 shows the first stage of upholstery, the inside back being webbed with three vertical and two horizontal webs with hessian stretched over, maintaining the hollow shaping of the back, by tensioning vertically but not horizontally. One web is sufficient for the inside arm to support the lining of hessian tacked on all four sides.

116

*Figure 67* Beech frame for
Victorian style button-back
chair

*Figure 68* Commencement of
upholstery of chair

*Figure 69* Groundwork for
upholstery of back of chair

*Figure 70* Back and arms of chair covered, seat first stuffed with stitching of edge in progress

Figure 69 shows the preparation of the back. Upholsterer's scrim is sewn on to the base hessian leaving a border of loose scrim around the top, sides and base of the back approximately 12 cm (5 in.) in from the edges. This border is filled with hair or fibre, and the loose scrim is pulled over and tacked on the outer edge of the back. This padding needs no stitching. With the padding around the edge of the back, there should be a flat 'well' in the centre area. The positions of buttons should be marked in this flat area with the button twines sewn at these points into the hessian with a running line as explained in the section on buttoning (page 84).

Before proceeding further with work on the back, the arms should be stuffed and covered in scrim, or alternatively, the top covering may be tacked on the outer edge of the back. This padding needs no stitching. skin wadding over the filling. After tacking home the covering, buttons should be sewn in the appropriate positions, the twines being taken through the hessian lining the arm. After marking positions of buttons on the reverse side of the covering, continue with the back. Ample filling should be applied to the back to give the buttons a good depth of 'sink'.

Figure 70 shows the back and arms covered, with the seat up to the 'first' stuffing stage. The 'blind' stitch has been inserted, the roll stitch is in progress, after which will come a top stitch to give a sharper 'pullover' type edge.

The seat has been sprung, with webs tacked on the underside of the seat members, $5 \times 4$ strands minimum supporting $9 \times 15$ cm ($3\frac{5}{8}$ to 6 in.) 10 S.W.G. (standard wire gauge) double cone springs. The springs should be cross-lashed with laid cord, using a good quality spring hessian on top. The tops of the springs should be sewn to the covering hessian.

The outside arms and outside back may be trimmed with ruche, tacked around the edge of the frame, or slip-stitched on the edges without trimming.

Diagram 78 shows the finished chair, trimmed with fringe around the base.

*Diagram 78* Button-back chair completed with fringe trimming

121

*Figure 71* Chair as purchased in need of new covering

122

# Restoration of a Victorian twist-leg chair

Figures 71, 72, 73 and 74 show an excellent example of the use of a hand-worked, wool embroidery replacing the original covering of a rather quaint, old, low-seated chair. As can be seen, it is now much more colourful and attractive, showing off to advantage the floral embroidered pattern, and enhanced value.

Figure 71 shows the original chair as purchased with the seat covering badly torn and back covering threadbare – reasons for being able to purchase the chair at a very reasonable cost at an antique furniture sale room.

The seat was completely stripped and re-upholstered with new webbing and hessian, re-using the original horse hair after a good teasing, and covering this with new calico as an under-covering, as described on pages 47 to 51.

Figure 72 shows completion of the embroidery of the seat covering before removal from the embroidery frame, showing shaping of the outline of the embroidery to fit the loose seat of the chair. This outline was marked from a template of the old seat covering.

*Figure 72* Completed embroidery for seat still on embroidery frame showing shaping of outline to fit loose seat of chair

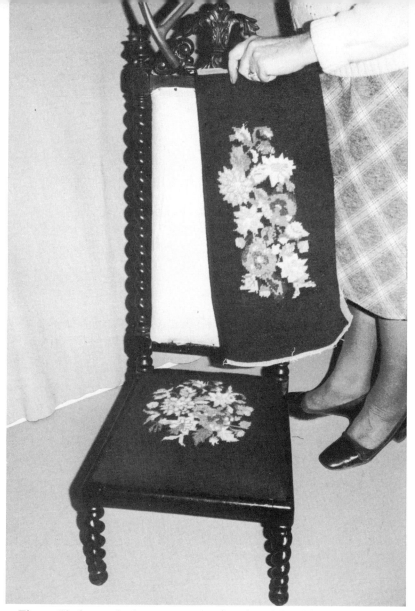

*Figure 73* Loose seat completed set in frame; ready for back covering to be tacked in position

Figure 73 shows the loose seat completed and fitted in the seat frame, with the back covering ready to be temporary tacked in place. The upholstery of the back, as is often the case, was in good condition, consequently the material used as an undercover was replaced and extra new wadding was laid over.

The outline of the embroidery for the back was sufficient to fold under and tack with gimp pins into the rebate on top and base of the back, finishing with oxidised, antiqued nails, which were space nailed. The sides of the back cover were tucked through between the leg twists and side of the back frame, tacking the covering on the outside back edge. The outside back covering was plain embroidery, joined down each side with matching wool, top and bottom using oxidised nails as the inside covering at the rebates. Figure 74 shows the completed chair.

*Figure 74* Completed chair

# Upholstery of bed headboards

Wooden bed headboards are, to my mind, one of life's tribulations when staying at a strange hotel or as an overnight guest at a friend's house. Usually a projecting moulding, or ledge, or the top edge of the headboard is strategically placed to catch the unwary back of the head when sitting up imbibing the early morning cup of tea. This discomfort can be overcome by a simple job of upholstery on the headboard.

Upholstering a bed headboard is relatively easy using foam and soft covering, or even P.V.C. covering, and may be upholstered completely plainly, float-buttoned, as in figure 75, or deeply buttoned, if you have a little more patience and courage. The advantage of using a P.V.C. covering is that it is spongeable and any grease or dye coming from the hair is easily and quickly removed.

Modern un-upholstered headboards are usually constructed from prefabricated board, mostly blockboard or chipboard, which has been coated with a painted finish or veneered with a plastic laminate or even wood veneer. This type of headboard will lend itself to easy upholstery, using either tacks or staples for fixing the covering.

*Figure 75* Bed headboard covered in velvet with float-buttoned finish

## Plain headboard

2.5 cm (1 in.) thickness foam will give an acceptable amount of padding for a plain type of finish, with the foam taken over the top and side edges to lose their sharpness. The foam should be held in position by applying adhesive to the underside of the foam in a band approximately 5 cm (2 in.) around the outer edges, and also to the board to prevent slippage downwards. The bottom line of the foam should terminate a short distance above the mattress line with the covering being folded under and tacked or stapled a little below this line. Covering should be finished on the outside of the board which, in turn, should be covered with a matching lining, slip-stitched around the edge.

The normal width of upholstery fabric (i.e. 122 to 127 cm [48 to 50 in.]) would be too narrow for a full-size double bed headboard, using a patterned fabric. In this case, the fabric would have to be extended by a join at each side. Alternatively, selection of a plain fabric would allow it to be run lengthwise across (selvedge edge), thus avoiding joining seams.

## Float-buttoned headboard

The float-buttoned headboard shown in figure 75 was not only an attractive design but was also particularly economic in covering material as it is made up of rectangular off-cuts of 'Dralon' velvet, with a soft foam interior.

In the example shown, the width of the headboard was divided into five sections and the height into three, with the lower section wider than the upper two to allow for the height of the mattress. The divided sections were then drawn on to the board and 0.5 cm ($\frac{3}{16}$ in.) holes drilled at positions where the lines cross to allow the buttoning twines to pass through.

3.6 cm ($1\frac{1}{2}$ in.) foam was cut slightly oversize and chamfered at the underside top and side edges, and was then placed in position. As the buttoning twines passed through the foam and board, it was unnecessary to use adhesive to hold the foam in position.

Individual sections of the covering were cut to size (allowing seaming on all sides) with a slight bowing outwards of the line at the machining lines to allow for the slight doming of each section. The outer edges of outer sections were cut to allow sufficient covering to tack at the rear of the board. In inserting the button ties, a running line of twine was passed through the tuft or wire loop of the button and taken through the hole in the headboard and tacked on the rear side. When doing this it is advisable to tack in a temporary fashion in the first instance, and, when satisfied that the buttons and lines are acceptable, the twines can be tacked permanently. The reverse side was covered in a matching lining.

## Deep-buttoned headboard

The base of the Queen Anne style headboard shown in figure 76 was cut from 1.3 cm ($\frac{1}{2}$ in.) thickness plywood with padding of 3.6 cm ($1\frac{1}{2}$ in.)

*Figure 76* Bed headboard, Queen Anne style, with deep diamond buttoning covered in velvet

thickness foam. This was designed for a single 91.5 cm (3 ft) bed. The diamond buttoning positions were marked on the base board in the desired positions and 0.5 cm ($\frac{3}{16}$ in.) holes drilled to take the twines through. Medium density foam was used and cut to the shape of the backboard using the backboard as a template and cutting the foam fractionally oversize.

The formation of buttoning was reproduced on the foam by marking with a felt tip pen, and then punching 1.3 cm ($\frac{1}{2}$ in.) holes through the foam at the button positions using a short length of gas piping sharpened at one end. When doing this, rest the foam on a piece of plywood or flat timber to protect the cutting edge of the tube and to ensure a clean cut, and then push the piping on to the foam and tap sharply with a hammer.

The example shown in figure 76 being 91.5 cm (3 ft) width was able to be worked from the normal width of upholstery velvet. Wider headboards buttoned in this way would necessitate joins in the covering; these joins should run under the diamond pleating lines. The base line of buttoning should be approximately at the pillow line, as in figure 76.

Figure 52 (*see page 84*) shows the reverse side of the covering marked with tailor's chalk at button positions. The distance between markings on the covering should allow for fullness to form the pleats between the buttons, i.e. an additional 20 per cent over the distances marked on the headboard base.

# Glossary

**Abrasion** Wear of fabric by rubbing.

**Air vent** Circular brass or plastic fitting to allow circulation or escape of air.

**Animal glue** Traditional adhesive supplied in slab or bead form for melting down.

**Back-tacking** A method of attaching covering to hide tacks.

**Bayonet needle** Upholstery needle with triangular point.

**Beech** Hard, close-grained timber used for upholstery frame making.

**Bevelled edge** Removal of sharp edge of timber rail (*see* Chamfer).

**Bias cutting** Cutting fabric diagonally across threads at 45 degrees.

**Blind stitch** Stitches formed within the filling to consolidate the edge.

**Blued tacks** Good quality steel tacks.

**Bottoming** Lining tacked on underside of upholstery work.

**Braid** Decorative band of trimming.

**Bridle ties** Loops of twine to hold filling in place.

**Burlap** American term for hessian.

**Cabriole hammer** Small-faced upholsterer's hammer.

**Cabriole leg** Queen Anne style leg.

**Calico** A white cotton material used as undercovering for upholstery work.

**Cambric** Finely woven, waxed cotton cloth for feather cushions.

**Canvas** Coarse cloth woven from jute fibre (*see* Burlap).

**Cavities** Square or rectangular holes moulded in latex foam.

**Chamfer** Bevel on corner of timber.

**Chipboard** Fabricated board made from wood chips.

**Chip foam** Foam made from granulated waste polyether foam.

**Coil spring** Traditional type of upholstery spring.

**Coir fibre** Coarse filling from the coconut husk.

**Collar** Strip of material machined to covering around shaped cuts.

**Currier** Leather processor.

**D.I.Y.** Do-it-yourself amateur handicraft work.

**Density** Relating to quality of foam.

**Doming** Degree of rise in centre of cushion.

**Double cone spring** Traditional type of 'waisted' upholstery spring.

**Dowelled joint** Timber joint held together with wooden pegs and glued.

**Down** A filling made from the light, fluffy covering from the underside of water fowl.

**'Drop-in' seat** Loose seat to fit into rebate of dining chair or bedroom stool.

**Feathers** Filling for cushions comprising coarse chicken or duck feathers.

**Felt** Coarse filling, either cotton or jute fibres.

**Fibre** Coarse filling used for the first stuffing of upholstery.

**Fine tacks** Slender tacks used for light timber.

**Float buttoning** Buttons lightly pulled down into covering.

**Fluting** Method of machining covering to give filled channels.

**Fluting sleeve** Gadget for filling flutes.

**Flys** Extension pieces of hessian, etc., to economise with covering.

**Frilling** Even gathering of loose fabric.

**Fringe** Decorative trimming around the base of upholstered items.

**Full seat** Upholstered seat without cushion.

**Fullness** Surplus covering causing wrinkling.

**Gassing** Formation of air cells by chemical action in manufacture of foam.

**Gauge (spring)** Thickness of spring wire.

**'Gee' cramp** Wood cramp made from steel in the form of a 'G'.

**Gimp** Narrow decorative strip to hide tacks along a rebate.

**Gimp pins** Fine tacks with small heads supplied in various colours.

**Groundwork** Basic working at the commencement of buttoning.

**Hardwood** Close-grained timber suitable for upholstery frames.

**Hassock** Firm kneeling cushion.

**Hide pincers** Wide-jawed pincers for tensioning leather.

**Horse hair** Good quality filling for traditional upholstery.

**Impermeable** Air- and water-tight.

**Improved tacks** Tacks with larger heads than the fine version.

**Jute** A coarse fibre used in the weaving of hessian and webbing.

**Laid cord** Thick spring lashing cord made from flax or hemp fibres.

**Latex foam** Foam manufactured from sap from the rubber tree.

**Linen webbing** Good quality webbing woven from flax and cotton fibre.

**Lining** A thin, cotton fabric of various colours.

**Lip** Front edge of cushion seat.

**Loose seat** Detachable seat fitting into rebate of seat.

**Mitred** Joined diagonally.

**'Mole' grip** Specialised type of pliers.

**Motif** Figuring on fabric.

**Nap** Fabric surface with a 'brush'.

**No-Sag** Proprietary type of modern springing.

**Occasional chair** Chair suitable for differing occasions.

**Oxidized nails** Domed decorative nails with oxidized finish.

**P.V.A.** Poly Vinyl Acetate.

**P.V.C.** Poly Vinyl Chloride covering.

**Pin hammer** Light hammer for cabinet work.

**Pincore latex** Latex foam moulded with pencil-like holes.

**Pin-stuffed** An upholstered seat using one layer of filling only.

**Piping** Decoration to camouflage a machine seam.

**Plumed** *See* Fluting

**Plywood** Board manufactured with thin layers of wood laid at right-angles to each other.

**Polyether foam** Flexible foam produced by mixture of chemicals.

**Pouffe** Floor cushion generally made for fireside use.

**Prefabricated board** Sheet of wood made mechanically.

**Radius section** Part of frame with curved section.

**Rasp** Coarse file for timber.

**Rebate** A channel machined in timber frame for tacking covering.

**Reconstituted foam** *See* Chip foam.

**Refurbishing** Restoring.

**Regulate** To use regulator.

**Regulator** An upholsterer's needle with flat end for regulating filling.

**Resiliency** Amount of flexibility or springiness.

**Resilient webbing** Laminated rubber webbing.

**Ruche** Decorative trimming to hide machine line on covering.

**S.W.G.** Standard wire gauge.

**Sash cramp** Long bar with adjustable jaws to hold timber whilst being glued.

**Scrim** Material loosely woven to encase filling for stitching rolls, etc.

**Scroll arm** A shaped arm with a roll-over appearance.

**Second stuffing** Stuffing generally of better quality worked over the 'first' stuffing.

**Shoddy** A poor quality filling made from fibres from reclaimed waste materials.

**Show-wood frame** An upholstered frame with an amount of polished wood visible.

**Simulated leather** P.V.C., etc.

**Sinuous spring** Modern type of springing consisting of a continuous wire formed into 'U' shapes.

**Skewer** A long pin (7.5 to 10 cm [3 to 4 in.]) with end turned over into circle.

**Slabstock latex** Thin sheet latex without cavities.

**Slip knot** A knot made in twine tie which will 'slip' tight.

**Slip-stitching** Method of 'closing' joins in fabric on the job.

**Spoon back** A back with a concave inner surface.

**Spring needle** Heavy curved needle.

**Squab** Flat cushion generally firmly filled.

**Stay rail** A thin rail at the base of arm or back on an upholstery frame.

**Stile** A post in the construction of the frame interfering with the tuck through of covering.

**Stuffover** An upholstered frame with a completely covered appearance.

**Tack-roll** A method of softening a timber rail around the edge of seat, etc.

**Teasing** Opening of stuffing by working with the fingers.

**Template** A paper or card shape used for accurate cutting of covering.

**Temporary tacking**  The initial tacking process, leaving tacks protruding.

**Tenon**  The projecting piece of mortice and tenon joint.

**Tension spring**  An elongated small coil spring fixed at ends.

**Thumb-roll**  Tack-roll approximately the thickness of the thumb.

**Top stitch**  The final row of stitching to obtain a fine edge.

**Top stuffed**  Upholstery effected on the top surface of seat members.

**Walling**  Sticking thin sheet foam to eliminate unevenness of cavities.

**Well of seat**  Flat surface of seat to accept a cushion.

**Wings**  Projections at sides of back to provide head support.

**Wood-wool**  Shredded wood fibres.

**Zig Zag**  A proprietary form of sinuous springing formed from a series of 'U' bends.

# List of distributors of upholstery sundries

**U.K.**

**Aberkenfig Upholstery,** 5 Bridgend Road, Aberkenfig, Bridgend, Glam

**Acre Furnishing Services Ltd,** 38–40 Kennington Park Road, London SE11 4RS

**Andrews Upholstery,** 302 Oxford Road, Reading, Berks RG3 1ER

**Anglia Upholstery (Ipswich) Ltd,** Unit 12, Dedham Place Workshops, Water Works Street, Ipswich, Suffolk

**Antiques of Tomorrow,** 17 Tower Street, Rye, East Sussex TN31 7AU (*Polished and unpolished frames and velvet coverings only*)

**Aquarius Soft Furnishing,** 5a Hamilton House, Heath Road, Cox Heath, Maidstone, Kent

**C. Atkins,** 1 Union Street, Newport Pagnell, Bucks

**A. Baker & Son,** 71a Fore Street, Ipswich, Suffolk IP4 1JZ

**Barking Home Improvements,** 350 Ripple Road, Barking, Essex

**Barnes & Co (Materials),** Kangley Bridge Road, Sydenham, London SE26 5AX.

**Bedford Upholstery Service,** c/o Tina's, 139 Kettering Road, Northampton

**David Block,** 150 Station Road, Woburn Sands, Milton Keynes, Beds

**Bruno-Galetti Ltd,** 72 Haverstock Hill, London NW3 2BE

**Buxton Upholstery,** 5 Scarsdale Place, Buxton, Derbyshire SK17 6EF

**Coleman's,** 28-30 Market Street, Birkenhead, Cheshire

**Conway Furnishers,** 3–5 High Street, Dunmow, Essex CM6 1AB

**Coventry Foam and Upholstery Supplies,** 65–69 Coventry Street, Stoke, Coventry CV2 4ND

**Mr Crumpton,** 42 St. Neots Road, Sandy, Beds

**P. J. David & Son,** 16c Church Street, St. George's, Telford

**Dee Cee,** 27 Hayburn Road, Millbrook Estate, Southampton, Hants

**Dudley Home Interiors,** Vine House, Fair Green Reach, Cambridge

**The Easy Chair,** 30 Lyndhurst Road, Worthing, Sussex

**R. Eldridge,** 502 Portswood Road, Southampton, Hants SO5 3SA

**A. C. Fish,** Bullace Lane, r/o 82 High Street, Dartford, Kent

**Fourways Furnishings Ltd,** 5 Sevenoaks Road, Borough Green, Kent

**Fringe & Fabrics,** Station Road, Broxbourne, Herts

**Gem Upholstery,** 157 Southend Road, Grays, Essex RM17 5NP

**Gravesham Upholstery,** 4–5 East Milton Road, Gravesend, Kent

**W. A. V. Hallett (Furn.) & Son,** 53 High Street, Lee-on-Solent, Hants PO13 9BU

**W. E. Harryman,** 145 Half Moon Lane, Herne Hill, London SE24 9JY

**S. Hodgson,** 36 High Street, Shefford, Beds SG17 5DG

**Hornet Hardware,** 24 The Hornet, Chichester, West Sussex

**J. E. Janes,** 32 Clarence Road, Grays, Essex RM17 6QJ

**Jonmar Upholstery,** The Old Maltings, St Andrews Street South, Bury St. Edmunds, Suffolk

**K. & M. Upholstery,** 165 Luckwell Road, Bristol BS3 3HB

**Brian Kirby & Co.,** 154 Springfield Road, Brighton, Sussex BN1 6DG

**Local Trading Co.,** 207 London Road, Sheffield S2 4LJ

**Lowcross,** 33 High Street, Whitchurch, Shropshire

**D. M. McCartney (Furnishing),** 1 Mansfield Road, Baldock, Herts SG7 6EB

**W. Monks & Sons,** London Road, Sawbridgeworth, Herts

**Morgan Handyman Supplies,** 27 Carlton Road, Nottingham, Notts

**N. R. Neve,** 31 The Broadway, St. Ives, Hunts PE17 4BX

**A. C. Prickett & Sons Ltd,** 42 The Broadway, Leigh-on-Sea, Essex

**F. E. Puleston Co. Ltd,** r/o 148 Leagrave Road, Luton, Beds

**R. D. Upholstery,** 26 Elm Parade, Elm Park, Essex

**Re-Upholstery (Mr. Flood),** Trafalgar Street, Gillingham, Kent

**A. J. Roberts & Co. Ltd,** 8 Tudor Road, Cardiff CF1 8RF

**Russell Trading Co.,** 75 Paradise Street, Liverpool L1 3BP

**J. P. Shearn,** 9 Park Place, Dover, Kent

**Mr. A. Smith,** 5a High Street, Hadleigh, Suffolk

**Strand Upholstery,** 793 Southchurch Road, Southend-on-Sea, Essex

**Superease Upholstery,** 5 Hannah Street North, Rhondda, Glam

**I. R. Taylor,** 12 Malpas Road, Newport, Gwent NPT 5PA

**F. W. Tuck,** Russells Yard, Bell Street, Great Baddow, Essex

**F. H. Watts Ltd,** The Handyman Centre, 111 Shirley Road, Southampton, Hants

**H. D. Winslow,** 460 London Road, Westcliff-on-Sea, Essex SSO 9LA

**Yeovil Upholsteries D.I.Y. Supply Centre,** 9 Wyndham Street, Yeovil, Somerset


## U.S.A.

Some of the firms listed below may sell only wholesale or in bulk quantities. Request the name of a distributor in your area. For an alternative source, contact a local upholsterer who can probably sell you what you need.

### Fabric

**Crompton-Richmond Co., Inc,** 1071 Avenue of the Americas, New York, N.Y. 10018

**Ford Motor Co.,** Chemical Products Div., 3001 T Miller Road, Dearborn, Mich. 48120

**F. Schumacher & Co,** 939 Third Avenue, New York, N.Y. 10022

**J. P. Stevens & Co,** 1185 Avenue of the Americas, New York, N.Y. 10036

### Fiber

**Blocksom & Co,** 406 Center Street, Michigan City, Ind. 46360

**Duracote Corp.,** 358 N. Diamond Street, Ravenna, Ohio 44266

**Excelsior, Inc.,** 726 Chestnut Street, Rockford, Ill. 61102

**International Textile, Inc.,** 2610 N. Pulaski Road, Chicago, Ill. 60639

**Universal Fibres, Inc.,** 65 9 Street, Brooklyn, N.Y. 11215

### Foam

**Accurate Foam Co.,** 819 Fox Street, La Porte, Ind. 46350

**Fairmont Corp.,** 625 N. Michigan Avenue, Chicago, Ill. 60611

**Firestone Foam Products Co.,** 823 Waterman Avenue, P.O. Box 4159, E. Providence, R.I. 02914

**Foamage, Inc.,** 506 S. Garland, Orlando, Fla. 32801

**Perma Foam, Inc.,** 605-R 21 Street, Irvington, N.J. 07111

### Springs

**Barber Mfg. Co., Inc.,** 1824 Brown Street, P.O. Box 2454, Anderson, Ind. 46016

**Dudek & Bock Spring Mfg. Co.,** 5102 W. Roosevelt Road, Chicago, Ill. 60650

**Select-A-Spring Corp.,** 190 Railroad Avenue, Jersey City, N.J. 07302

**Starcraft Mfg. Co.,** 16918 Edwards Road, Cerritos, Calif. 90701

# Index